GRADE 08 KEYBOARDS

Published by
Trinity College London Press
trinitycollege.com

Registered in England
Company no. 09726123

Photography by Zute Lightfoot, lightfootphoto.com

© Copyright 2017 Trinity College London Press
Second impression, November 2017

Unauthorised photocopying is illegal
No part of this publication may be copied or reproduced in any form or by any means without the prior permission of the publisher.

Printed in England by Caligraving Ltd.

THE EXAM AT A GLANCE

In your exam you will perform a set of three songs and one of the session skills assessments. You can choose the order of your set list.

SONG 1

Choose a song from this book.

SONG 2

Choose *either* a different song from this book
or a song from the list of additional Trinity Rock & Pop arrangements, available at trinityrock.com
or a song you have chosen yourself: this could be your own cover version or a song that you have written. It should be at the same level as the songs in this book and match the parameters at trinityrock.com

SONG 3: TECHNICAL FOCUS

Song 3 is designed to help you develop specific and relevant techniques in performance. Choose one of the technical focus songs from this book, which cover two specific technical elements.

SESSION SKILLS

Choose *either* **playback** *or* **improvising**.

Session skills are an essential part of every Rock & Pop exam. They are designed to help you develop the techniques music industry performers need.

Sample tests are available in our *Session Skills* books and free examples can be downloaded from trinityrock.com

ACCESS ALL AREAS

GET THE FULL ROCK & POP EXPERIENCE ONLINE AT TRINITYROCK.COM

We have created a range of digital resources to support your learning and give you insider information from the music industry, available online. You will find support, advice and digital content on:

- Songs, performance and technique
- Session skills
- The music industry

You can access tips and tricks from industry professionals featuring:

- Bite-sized videos that include tips from professional musicians on techniques used in the songs
- 'Producer's notes' on the tracks, to increase your knowledge of rock and pop
- Blog posts on performance tips, musical styles, developing technique and advice from the music industry

JOIN US ONLINE AT:

         and at **TRINITYROCK.COM**

CONTENTS

ALADDIN SANE	5	
BIRDLAND	15	
BOOGIE ON REGGAE WOMAN	24	
FIRTH OF FIFTH	32	TECHNICAL FOCUS
MY BABY JUST CARES FOR ME	42	
PEACHES EN REGALIA	51	TECHNICAL FOCUS
EXOGENESIS: SYMPHONY PART 2	56	
READY WEDNESDAY	64	TECHNICAL FOCUS
HELP PAGES	76	

THE AUDIO

Professional demo & backing tracks can be downloaded free, see inside cover for details.

Music preparation and book layout by Andrew Skirrow for Camden Music Services
Music consultants: Nick Crispin, Chris Walters, Christopher Hussey, Julie Parker
Drums recorded by Cab Grant and Jake Watson at AllStar Studios, Chelmsford
All other audio arranged, recorded & produced by Tom Fleming & Jeff Leach
Keyboard arrangements by Imogen Hall, Christopher Hussey, Mal Maddock, Andy Rapps & Jane Watkins

Musicians
Keyboards: Christopher Hussey, Jeff Leach
Bass: Tom Fleming, Sam Burgess
Drums: George Double
Guitar: Tom Fleming
Vocals: Alison Symons, Tom Adamson, Brendan Reilly
Cello: Sophie Gledhill
Harmonica: Stuart 'Son' Maxwell

YOUR PAGE
NOTES

ALADDIN SANE DAVID BOWIE

WORDS AND MUSIC: DAVID BOWIE

08 GRADE
KEYBOARDS

SINGLE BY
David Bowie

ALBUM
Aladdin Sane

RELEASED
13 April 1973

RECORDED
January 1973, Trident Studios, London, England

LABEL
RCA

WRITER
David Bowie

PRODUCERS
Ken Scott
David Bowie

Born in London, England, David Bowie was one of the most influential musical figures in rock and pop, as well as one of its most successful. His career spanned more than 50 years and involved numerous stylistic reinventions and innovations. Eleven of his albums reached No. 1 in the UK, including his final album, 2016's *Blackstar*, released two days before his death.

David Bowie's sixth album, *Aladdin Sane*, was released in 1973 and was his first No. 1 album in the UK. A pun on 'a lad insane' and inspired by Bowie's half-brother Terry, who was diagnosed as schizophrenic and eventually institutionalised, this is the album that introduced the iconic image of Bowie with a red and blue lightning bolt painted across his face on the cover. The experimental title song features a piano solo by Mike Garson, whose first two attempts were rejected by Bowie for being too conventional. Asking him to play something closer to 'avant-garde jazz', the improvised solo was recorded in one take. Garson:

> I've had more communication in the last 26 years about that one solo than the 11 albums I've done on my own, the six that I've done with another group that I'm co-leader of, hundreds of pieces I've done with other people and the 3,000 pieces of music I've written to date.

⚡ PERFORMANCE TIPS

The main challenge in this song is to devise a solo that will capture the spirit of Mike Garson's seminal improvisation on the original version. For ideas, listen to some of Garson's jazz recordings featuring note clusters, bitonality and other avant-garde effects. Throughout the song, observe all accidentals carefully as these are key to the distinctive and unsettling tonality.

ALADDIN SANE

WORDS AND MUSIC: DAVID BOWIE

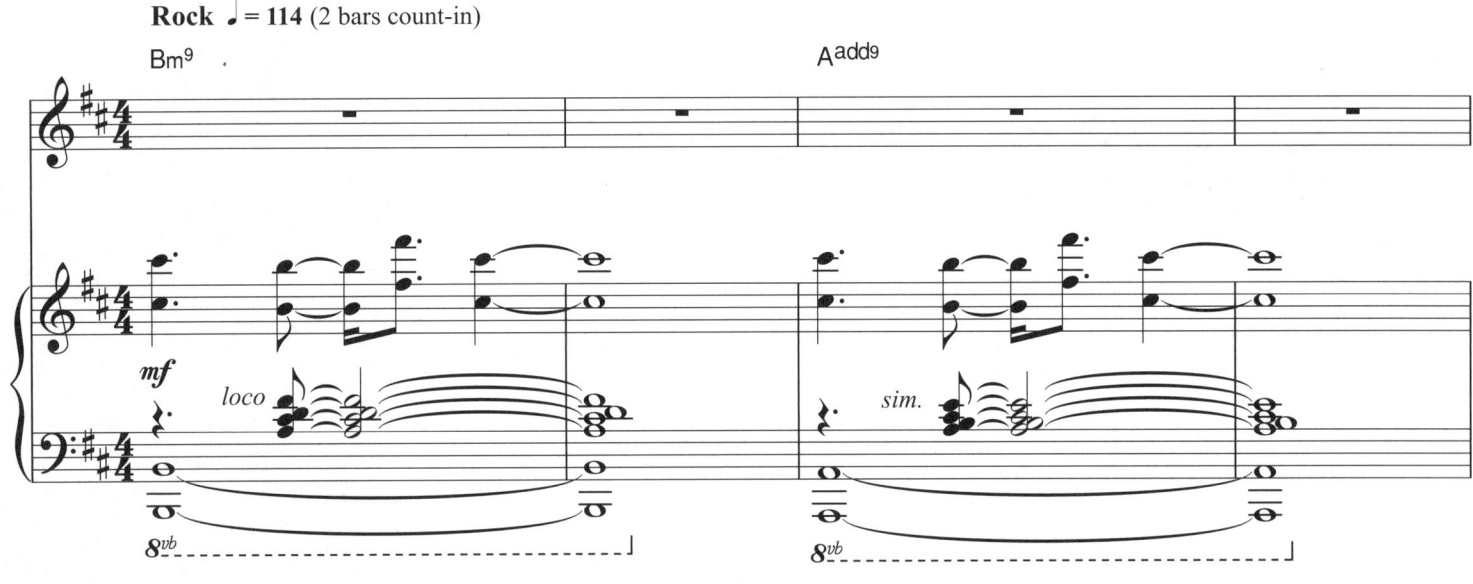

© 1973 Tintoretto Music
Chrysalis Music Limited, A BMG Company/RZO Music Limited/EMI Music Publishing Limited
All Rights Reserved. International Copyright Secured

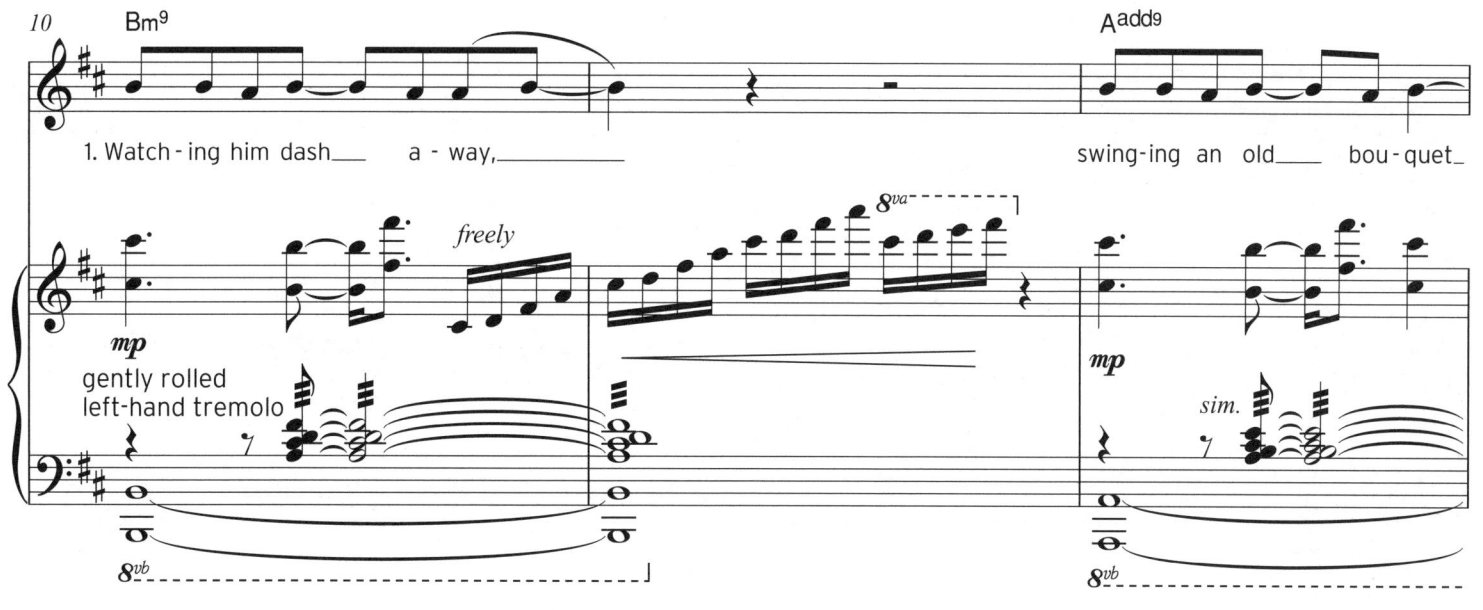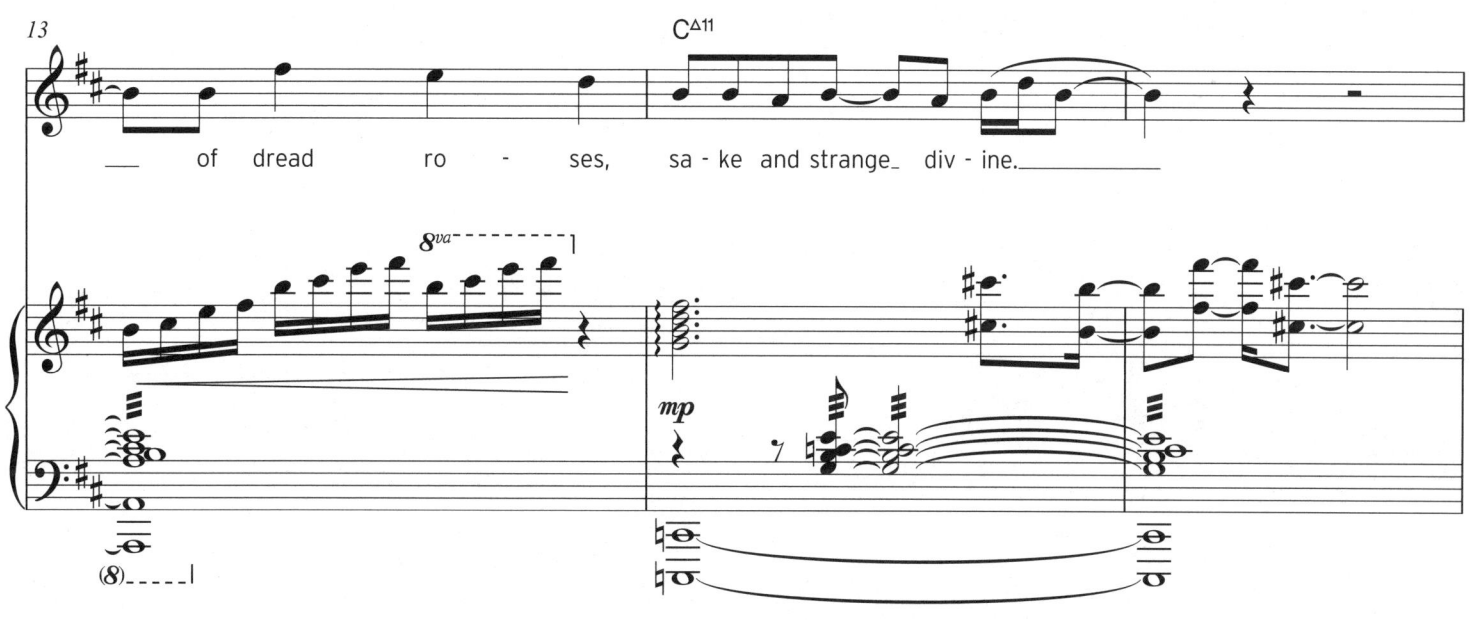

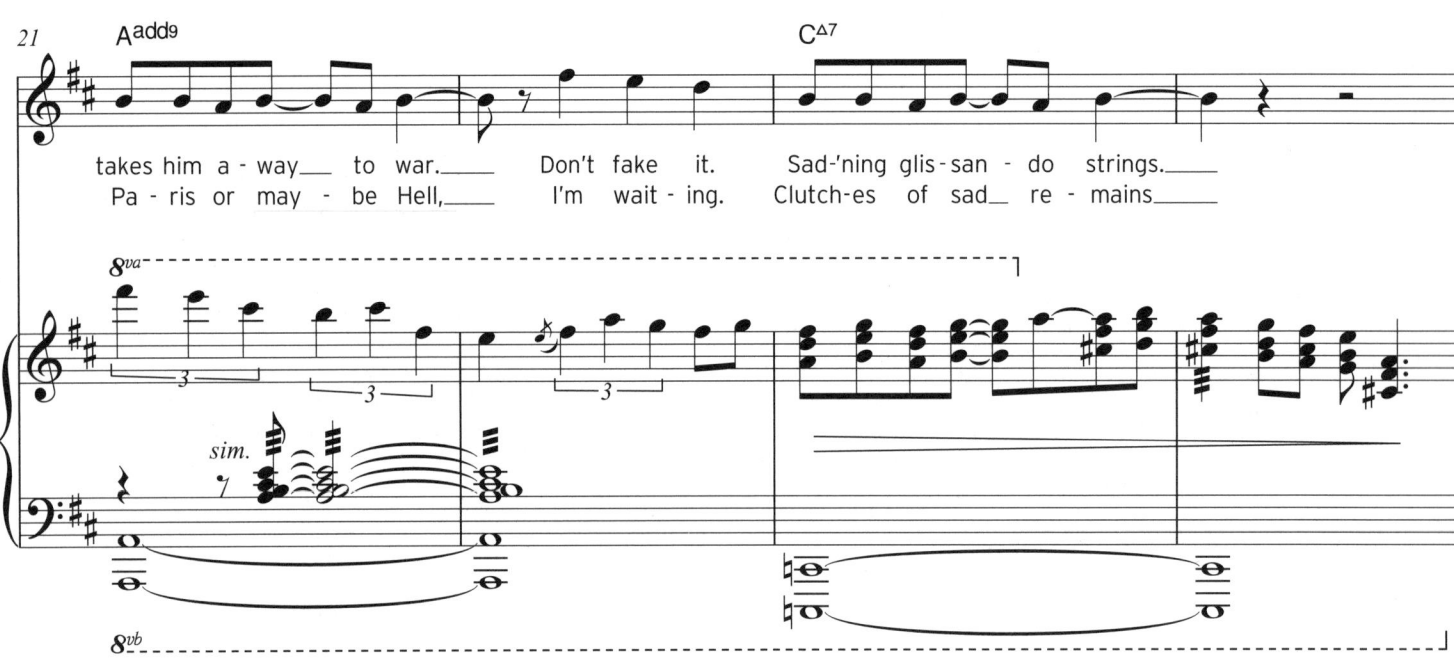
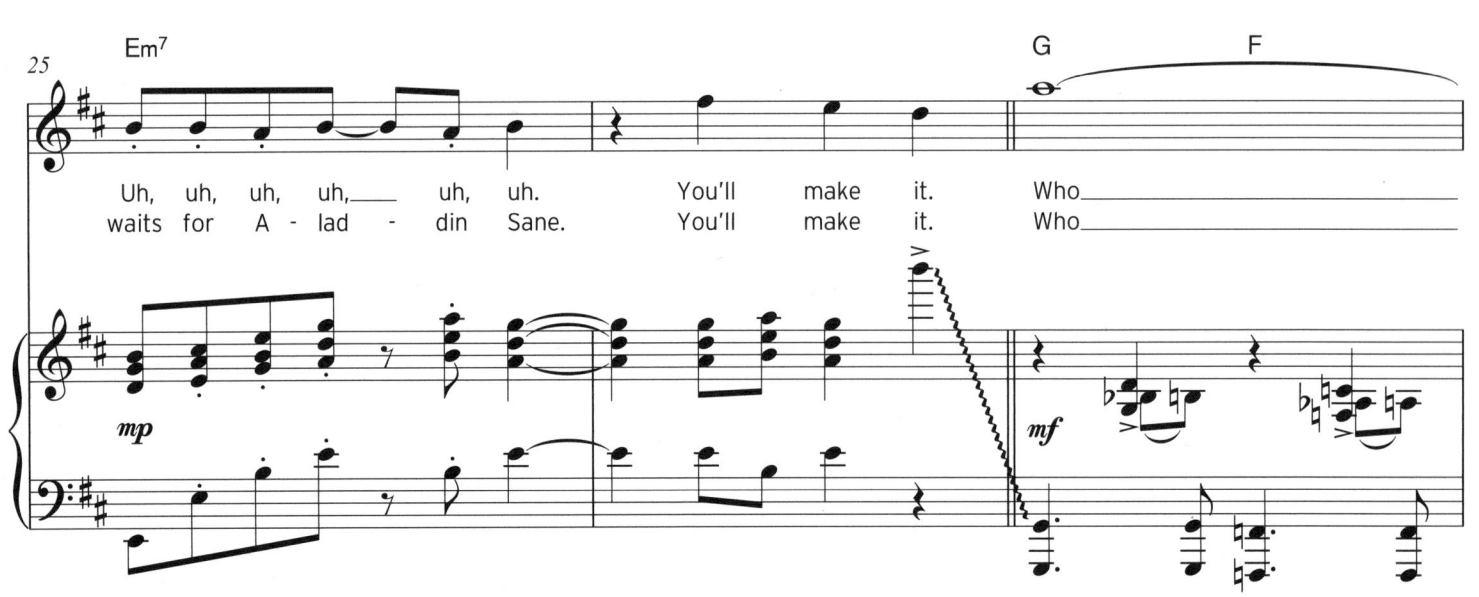

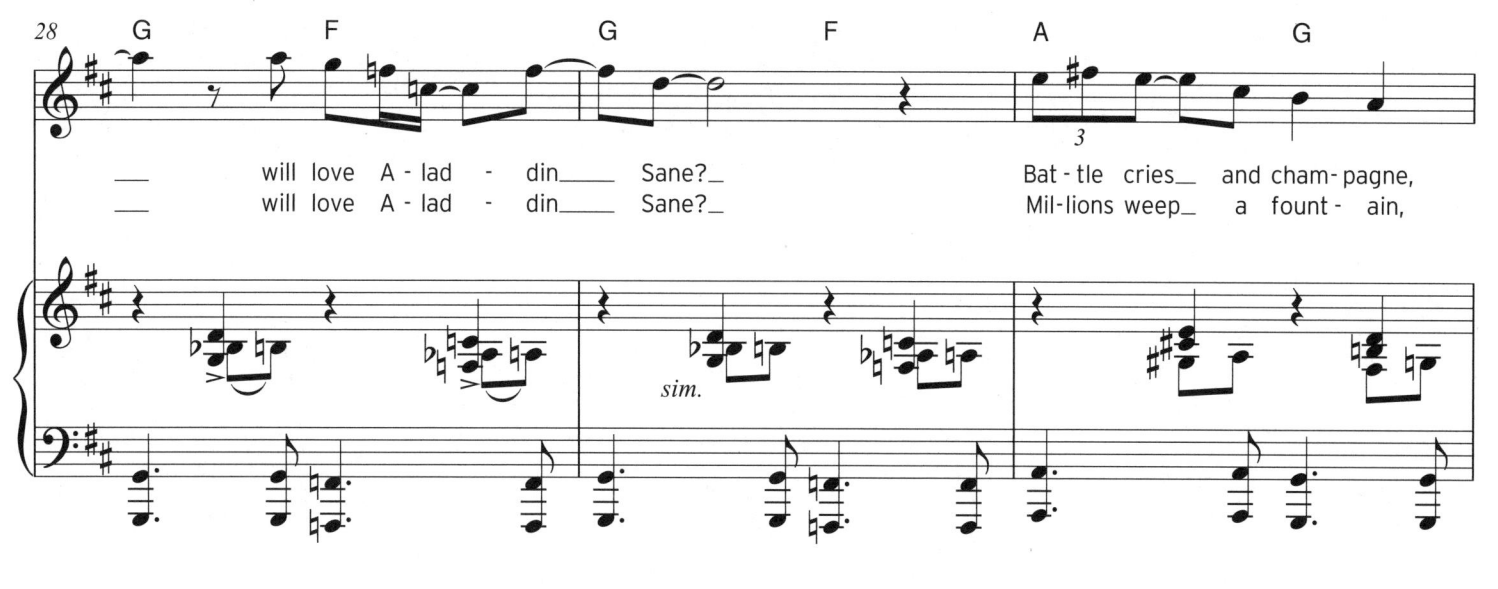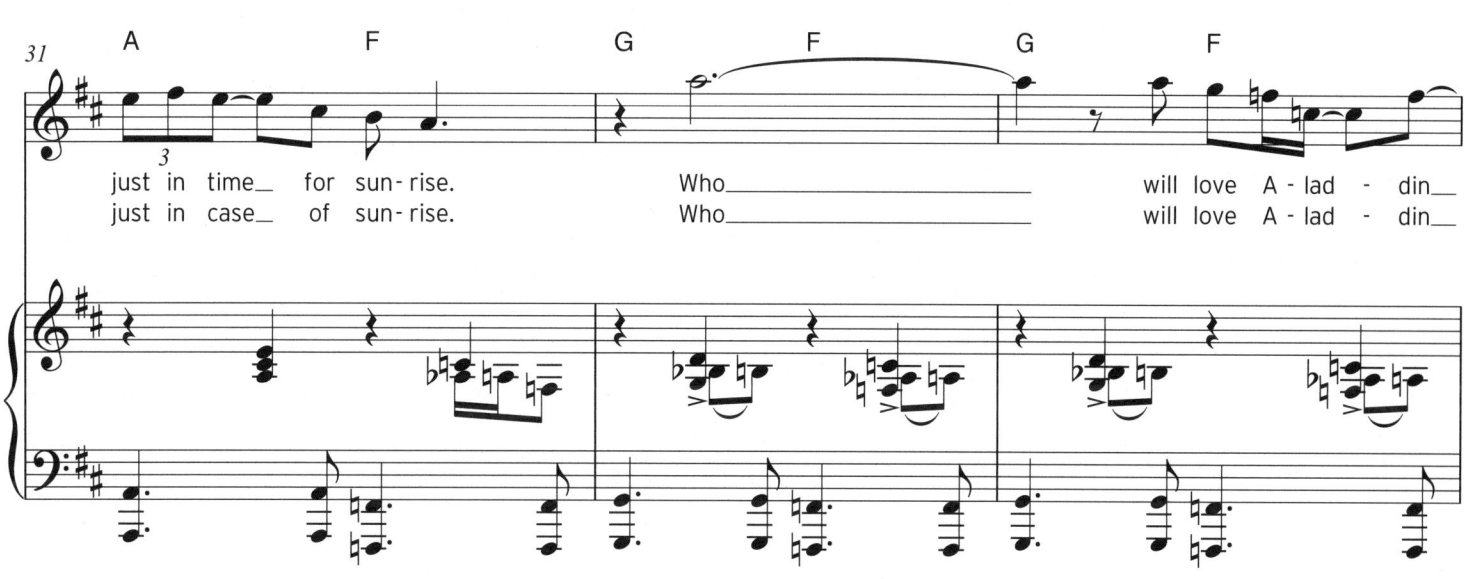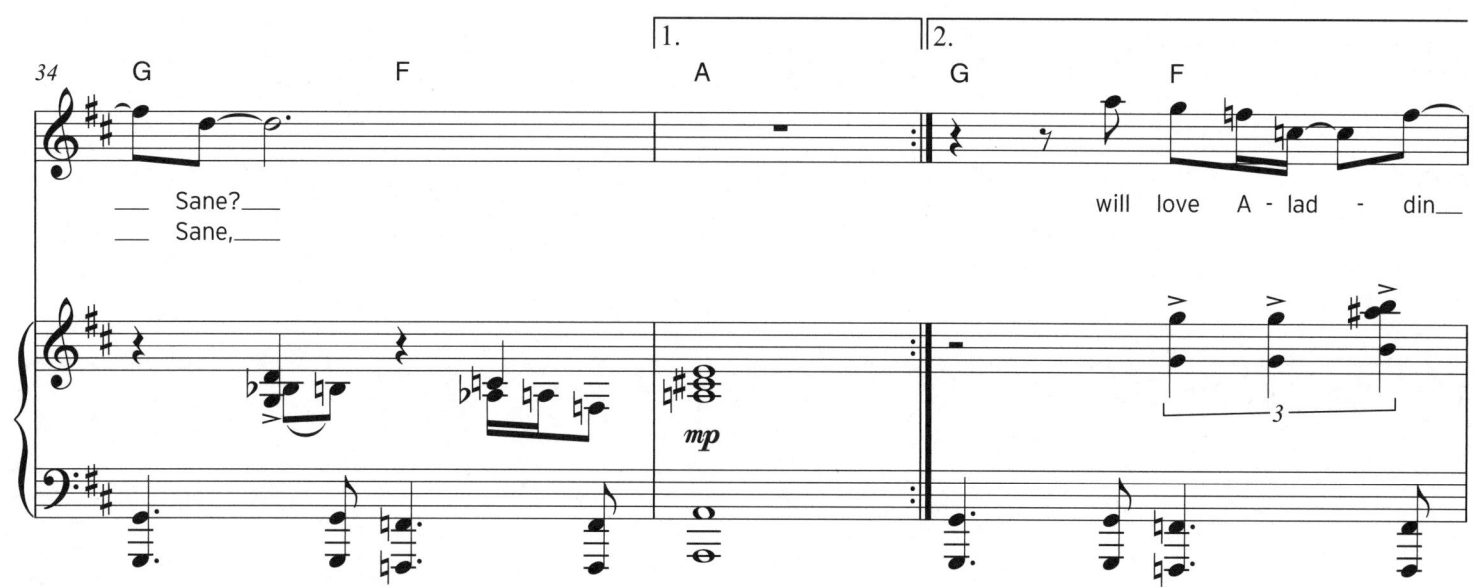

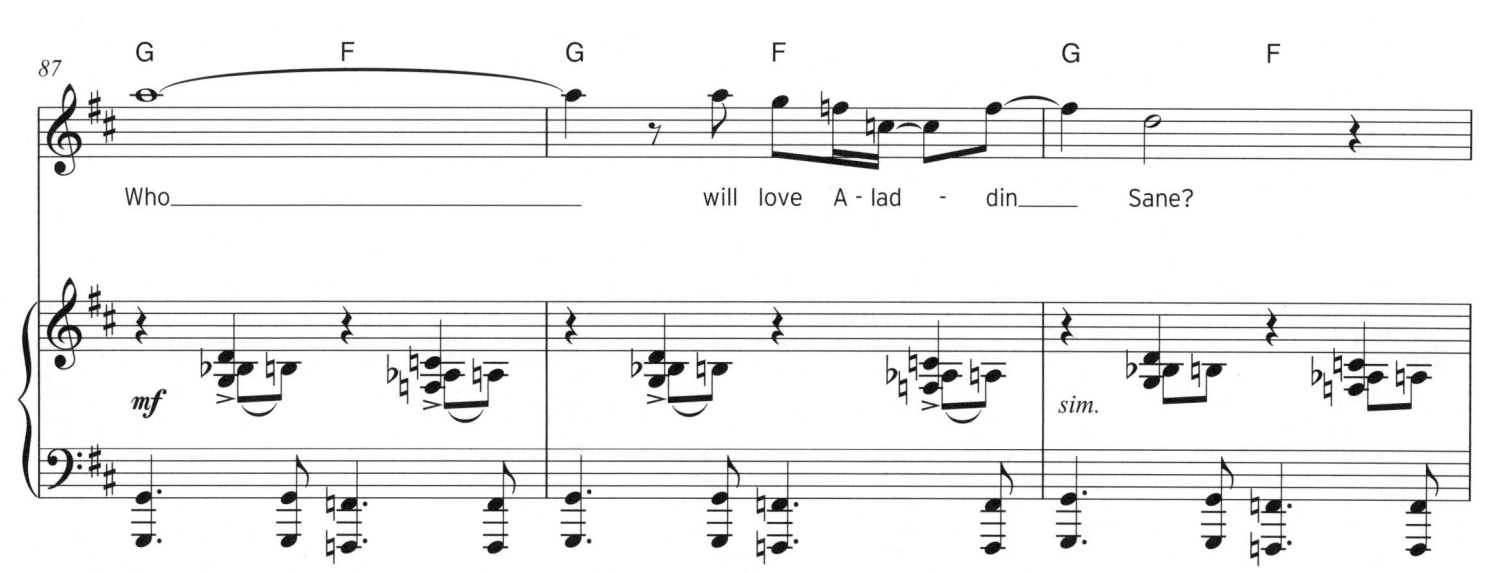

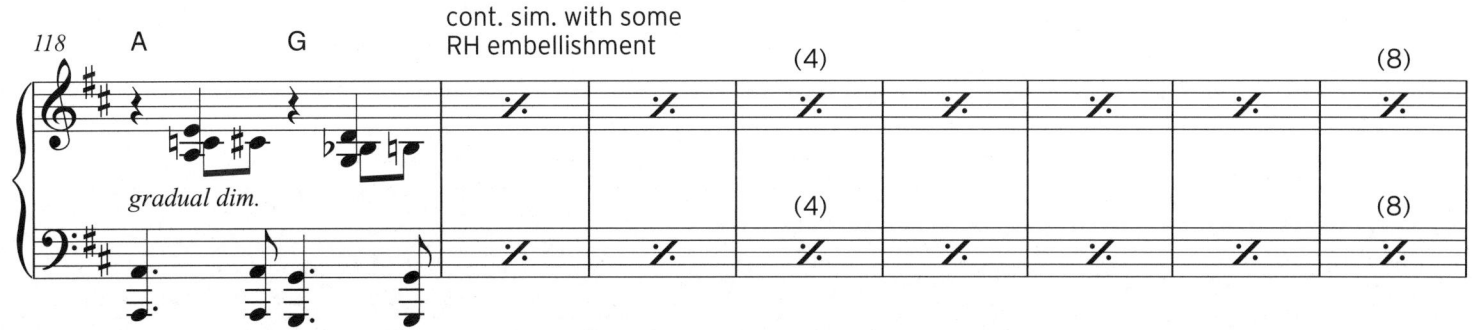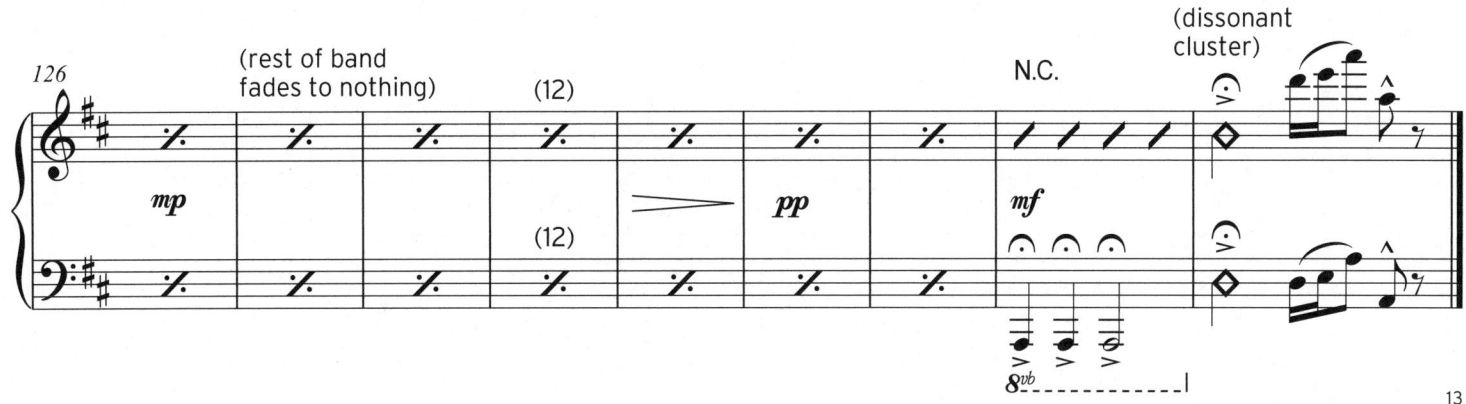

YOUR
PAGE
NOTES

BIRDLAND
WEATHER REPORT

WORDS AND MUSIC: JOE ZAWINUL

08 GRADE
KEYBOARDS

SINGLE BY
Weather Report

ALBUM
Heavy Weather

B-SIDE
A Remark You Made

RELEASED
March 1977 (album)

RECORDED
Devonshire Sound Studios, Hollywood California, USA

LABEL
Columbia

WRITER
Joe Zawinul

PRODUCERS
**Joe Zawinul
Jaco Pastorius
Wayne Shorter**

Weather Report was founded in 1970 by Joe Zawinul (keyboard) and Wayne Shorter (saxophone), former members of Miles Davis's studio band who played on 1969's *In a Silent Way* and 1970's *Bitches Brew*. Zawinul and Shorter were core members of a line-up that underwent many changes over the course of the band's 16-year existence.

Weather Report's acclaimed eighth album, 1977's *Heavy Weather*, proved to be the band's most commercially successful release, voted Album of the Year by leading jazz magazine *Down Beat*. Its opening instrumental piece, 'Birdland', was instantly recognised as a tour de force for the group, with Zawinul saying: 'When we rehearsed it the very first time it was easy to see that there was something special there. It's a wonderful feeling.' By this point the band also included bass virtuoso Jaco Pastorius, drummer Alex Acuña and percussionist Manolo Badrena. 'Birdland' was a tribute to the legendary New York jazz club of the same name. Zawinul said: 'I met Miles there, and Duke Ellington and Louis Armstrong. I met my wife Maxine there. Everyone I worshipped I met at Birdland.' Jon Hendricks set lyrics to it in 1980, and Manhattan Transfer won two Grammys for their vocal version.

⚡ PERFORMANCE TIPS

This song needs a strong sense of groove. To capture the right feel, listen closely to the detail of the accents, articulation and phrasing on the original track. The descending chromatic chords in bars 89-98 will need careful attention, and the section following this should convey a feeling of nervous anticipation, which is a challenge at the required soft dynamic. In fact, the whole song is a contrast between build-up and euphoric release, so aim to convey a feeling of joy when the release comes at bar 53 and elsewhere.

BIRDLAND

WORDS AND MUSIC: JOE ZAWINUL

© 1977 Mulatto Music, USA/Songs Of Universal Incorporated
Universal/MCA Music Limited
All Rights Reserved. International Copyright Secured

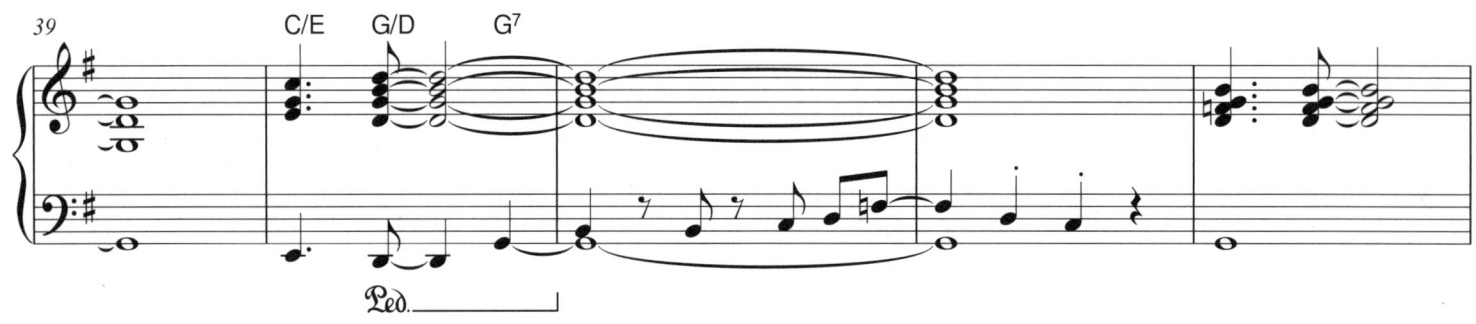
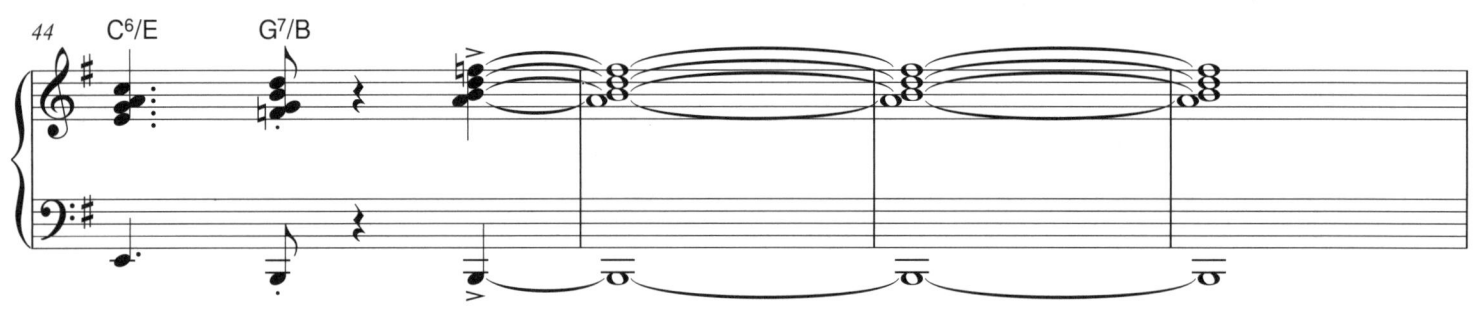

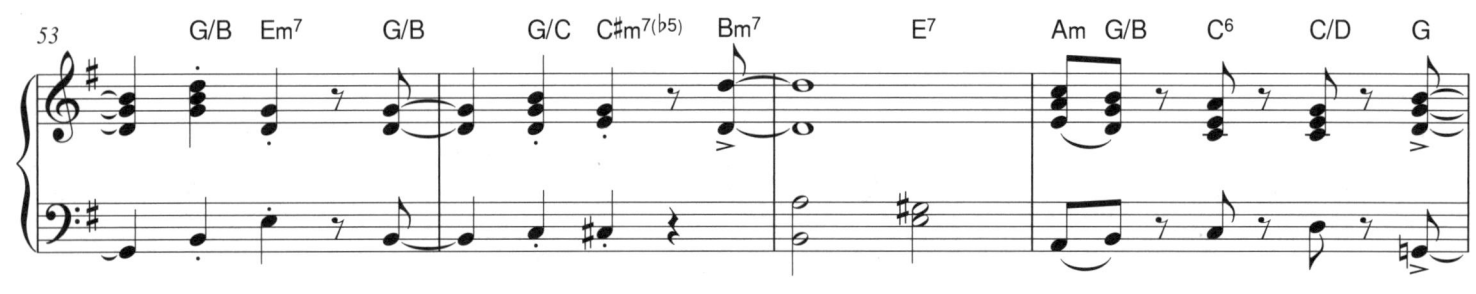

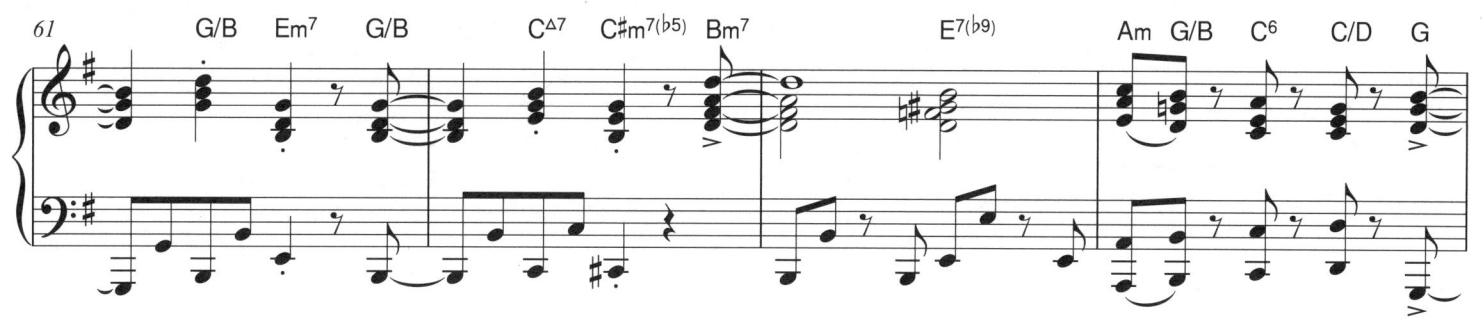
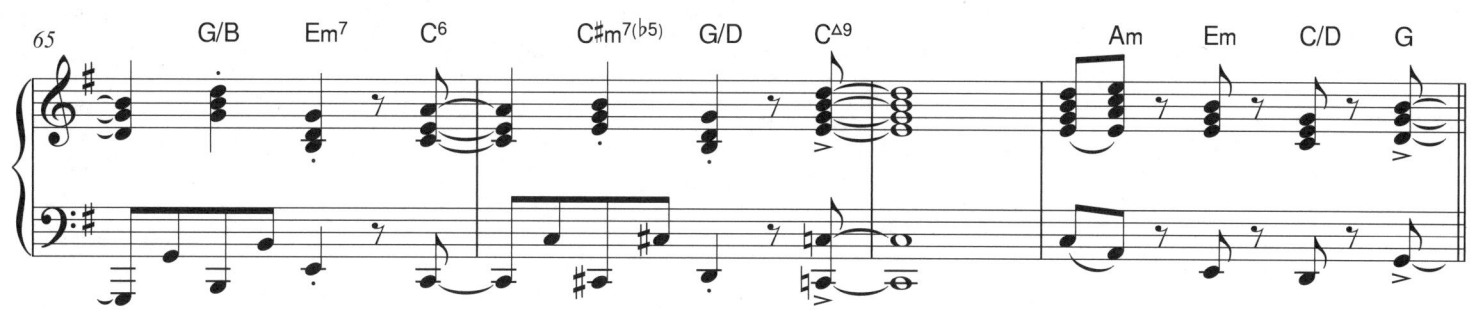

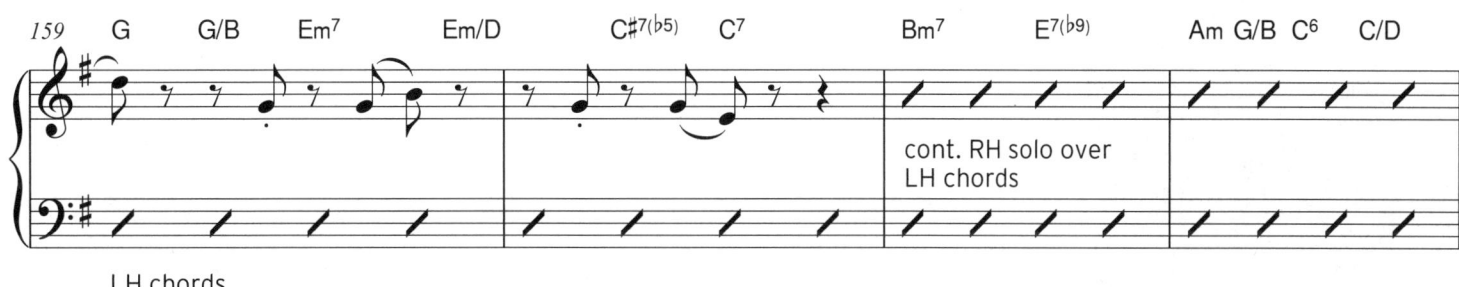
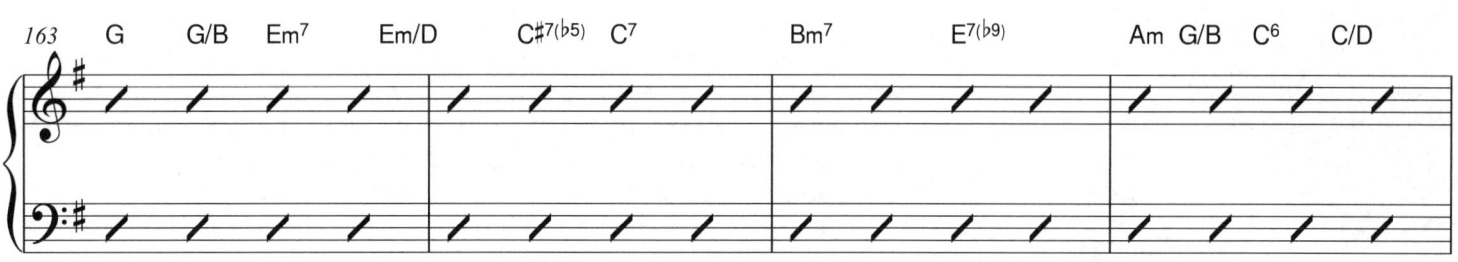
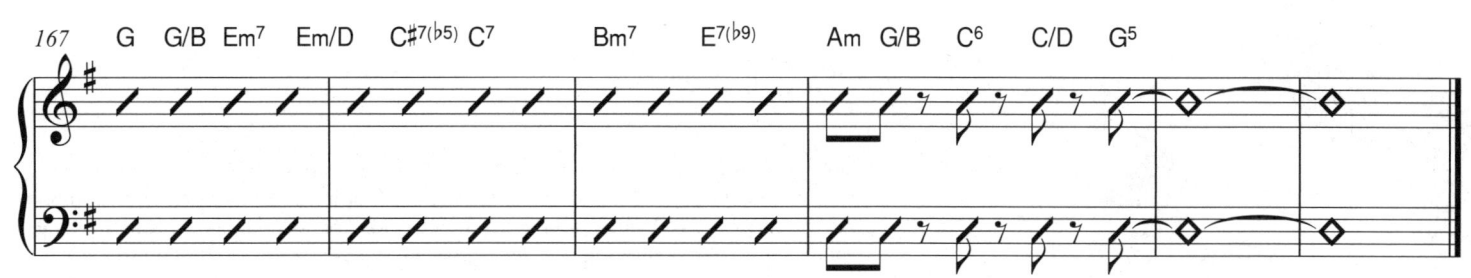

GRADE **08**
KEYBOARDS

SINGLE BY
Stevie Wonder

ALBUM
Fulfillingness' First Finale

B-SIDE
Seems So Long

RELEASED
**22 July 1974 (album)
November 1974 (single)**

RECORDED
**1973-1974, Record Plant, Los Angeles, California, USA
Westlake Recording Studios, Los Angeles, California, USA
Media Sound Recording Studios, New York City, New York, USA
Electric Lady, New York City, New York, USA (album)**

LABEL
Tamla

WRITER
Stevie Wonder

PRODUCERS
**Stevie Wonder
Robert Margouleff
Malcolm Cecil**

BOOGIE ON REGGAE WOMAN
STEVIE WONDER

WORDS AND MUSIC: STEVIE WONDER

Legendary American musician Stevie Wonder is a singer, songwriter, multi-instrumentalist and producer who has had 27 top-ten hits in the US since his first hit single 'Fingertips – Part 1 & 2' reached No. 1 in 1963 when he was just 13 years old.

'Boogie On Reggae Woman' is from Stevie Wonder's 1974 album *Fulfillingness' First Finale*, his seventh LP of the 1970s. It was his second No. 1 album in the US and first since suffering a serious head injury caused by a road accident the previous August. While on the way to a gig one afternoon, the car in which he was being driven crashed into the back of a truck and the resulting collision put Wonder into a coma for several days. 'What happened to me was a very, very critical thing, and I was really supposed to die,' he said. 'Boogie On Reggae Woman' followed the album's first single, the US No. 1 'You Haven't Done Nothin'', peaking at No. 3. The only musician other than Wonder on the track is conga player Rocky Dzidzornu, who also played on The Rolling Stones' 'Sympathy for the Devil'. The song earned Wonder a Grammy for Best R&B Vocal Performance, while *Fulfillingness' First Finale* won Album of the Year.

⚡ PERFORMANCE TIPS

Slow, detailed practice is probably the best way to approach learning this song, which is packed full of intricate licks and fills. Aim for a relatively light and nimble touch with neat and consistent grace notes. This song should be played with a piano sound in the right hand and synth bass in the left if this combination is available to you. Most importantly, try to capture Stevie Wonder's trademark joyful spirit by performing your carefully practised notes with a sense of spontaneity and freedom.

BOOGIE ON REGGAE WOMAN

WORDS AND MUSIC:
STEVIE WONDER

Funk soul ♩ = 107 (1½ bars count-in)

© 1974 (Renewed 2002) JOBETE MUSIC CO., INC. and BLACK BULL MUSIC c/o EMI APRIL MUSIC INC.
All Rights Reserved. International Copyright Secured. Used by Permission
Reprinted by permission of Hal Leonard LLC

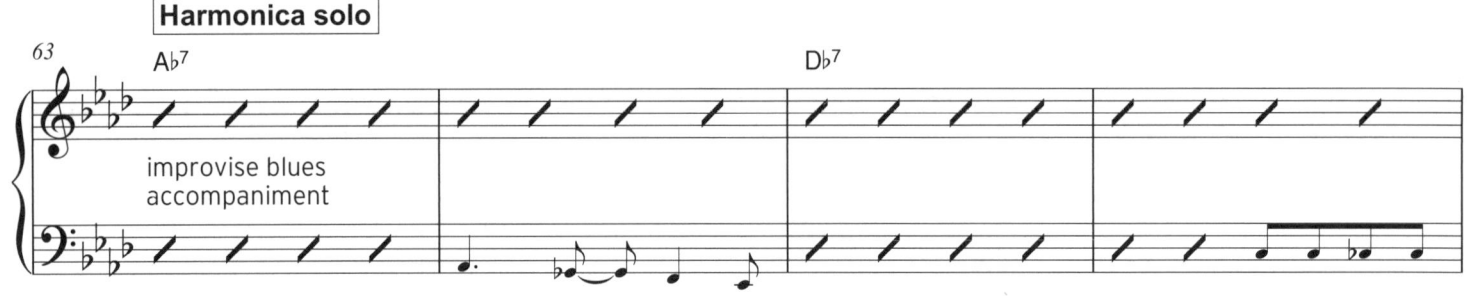
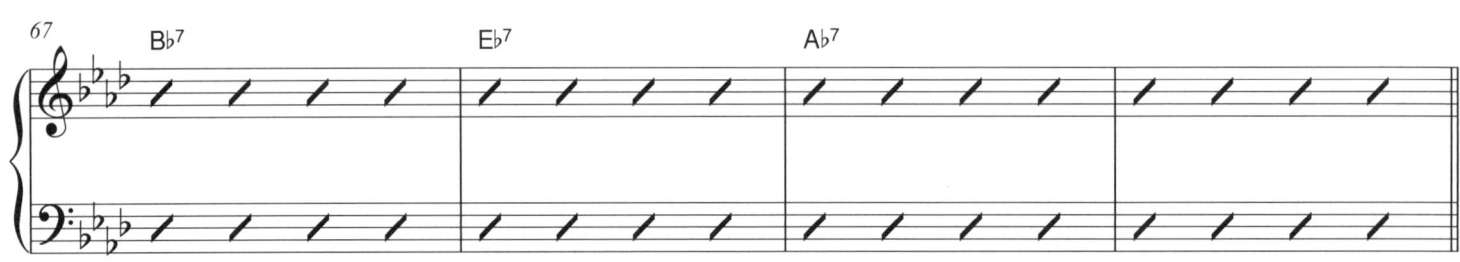

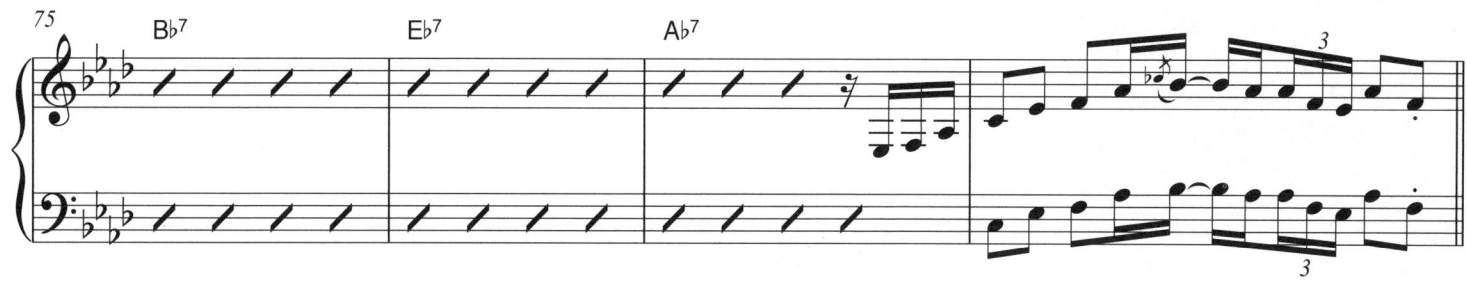

GRADE 08 KEYBOARDS

SINGLE BY
Genesis

ALBUM
Selling England by the Pound

RELEASED
13 October 1973

RECORDED
August 1973, Island Studios, London, England

LABEL
Charisma
Atlantic

WRITERS
Tony Banks
Phil Collins
Peter Gabriel
Steve Hackett
Mike Rutherford

PRODUCERS
John Burns
Genesis

TECHNICAL FOCUS

FIRTH OF FIFTH
GENESIS

WORDS AND MUSIC: TONY BANKS, PHIL COLLINS
PETER GABRIEL, STEVE HACKETT
MIKE RUTHERFORD

Formed in 1967, English rock group Genesis' line-up by the early 1970s consisted of Peter Gabriel (vocals, flute, oboe), Tony Banks (keyboard, guitar), Mike Rutherford (guitar, bass), Steve Hackett (guitar) and Phil Collins (drums). Gabriel left the band in 1975 for a successful solo career, replaced by Collins on vocals.

Widely considered one of prog rock's greatest pieces, 'Firth of Fifth' is from Genesis' fifth album, 1973's *Selling England by the Pound*. It was the band's most commercially successful album up to that point, featuring their first hit single 'I Know What I Like (In Your Wardrobe)'. The mostly instrumental, almost ten-minute-long 'Firth of Fifth' follows that song on the album, the music of which was mainly written by Banks and initially presented to the band for consideration on their previous album, 1972's *Foxtrot*, but didn't make the cut. Reworked for its follow-up, it features a rhythmically complex solo piano introduction before shifting through several different sections. Banks said:

> I was pretty pleased with that at the time… it had lots of bits in it. That's the sort of thing you get out of a group, I think, it leads you to places you weren't perhaps otherwise going to go.

TECHNICAL FOCUS

Two technical focus elements are featured in this song:

- Changing time signatures
- Semiquaver triplets

The opening section of this song is defined by **changing time signatures**, and you'll need to keep consistent semiquavers in mind to ensure that a steady flow is maintained. The **semiquaver triplets** in bars 21 and 23 are particularly challenging, representing the first time that the music has strayed away from flowing semiquavers. Count these carefully and aim for neat transitions between the triplets and the normal semiquavers.

TECHNICAL FOCUS
FIRTH OF FIFTH

WORDS AND MUSIC:
TONY BANKS, PHIL COLLINS, PETER GABRIEL
STEVE HACKETT, MIKE RUTHERFORD

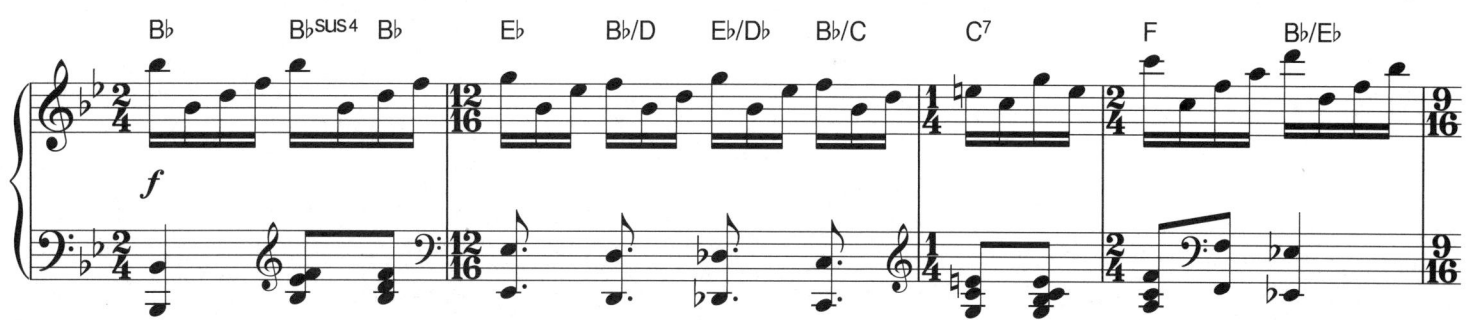

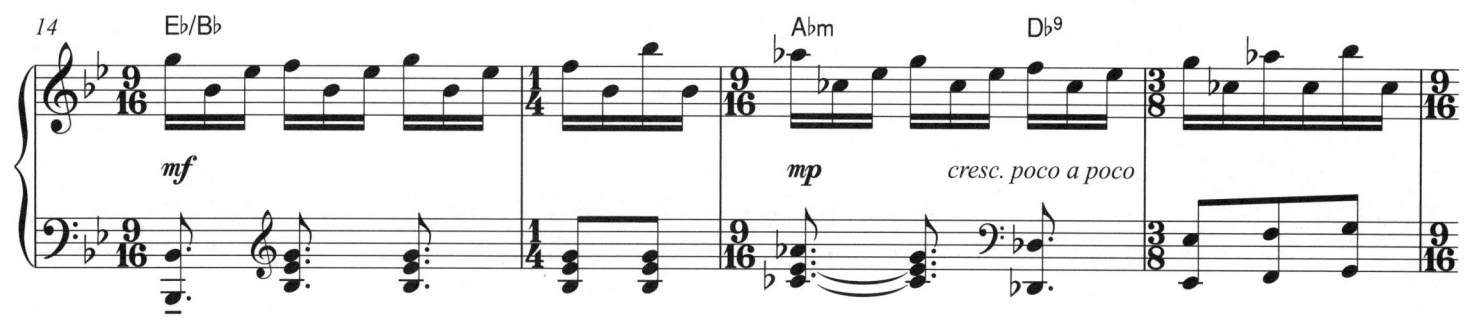

© 1973 Philip Collins Limited/Michael Rutherford Publishing Limited/Real World Music Ltd/Imagem Music BV/Stephen Hackett Limited
Imagem Music/EMI Music Publishing Limited
All Rights Reserved. International Copyright Secured

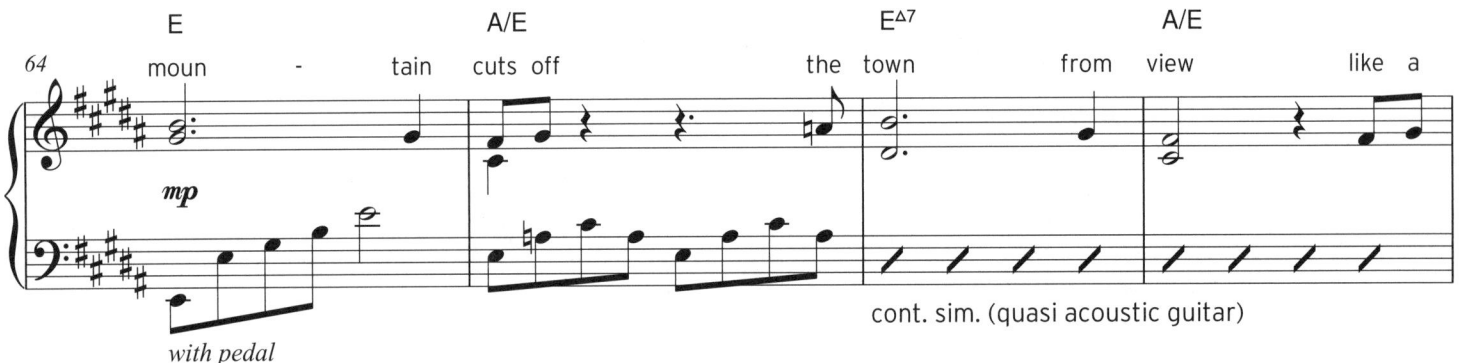

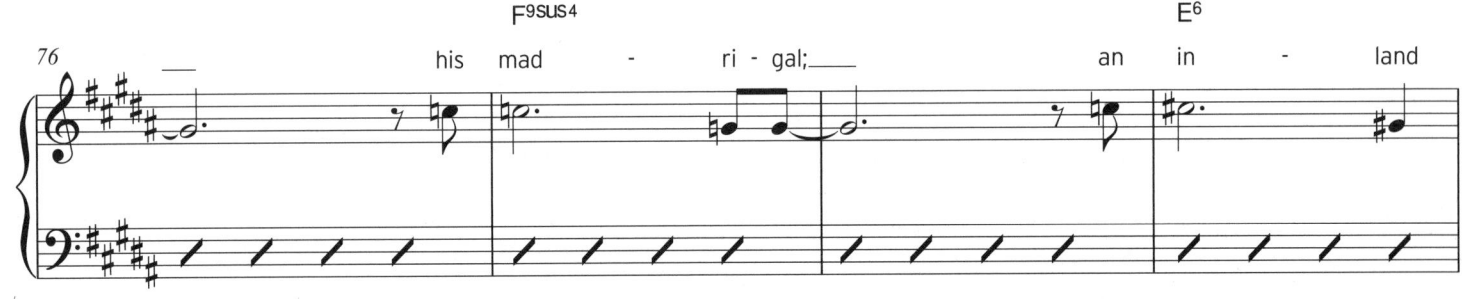

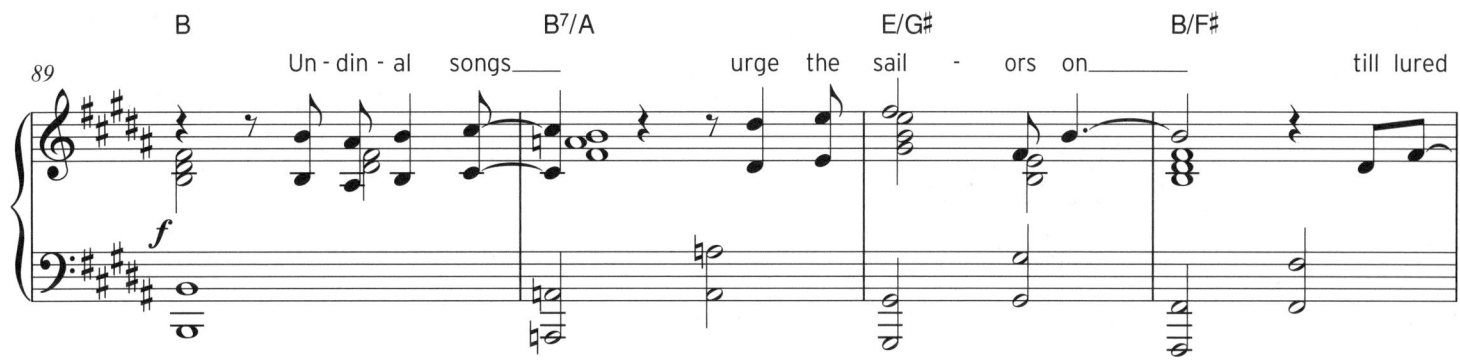
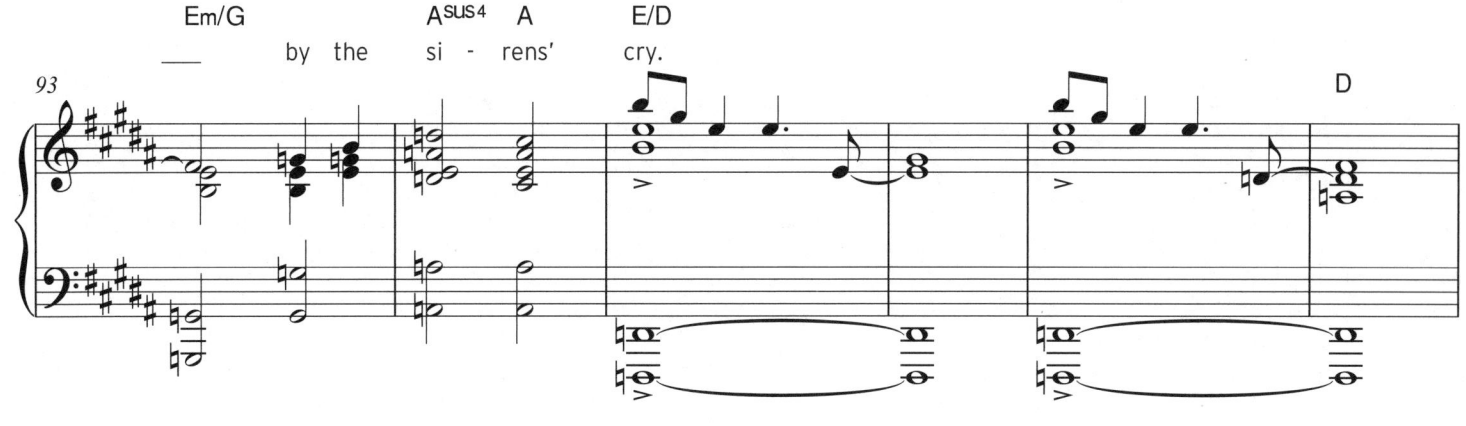

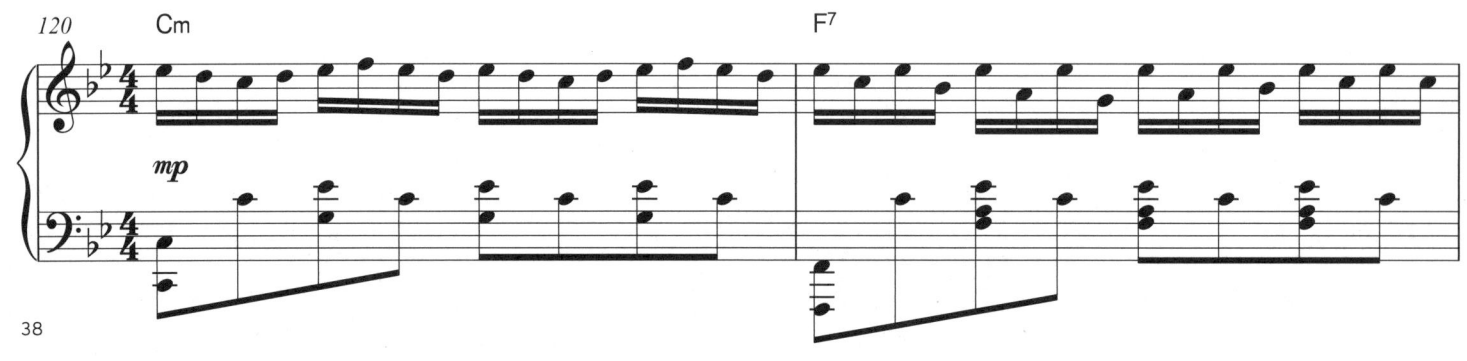

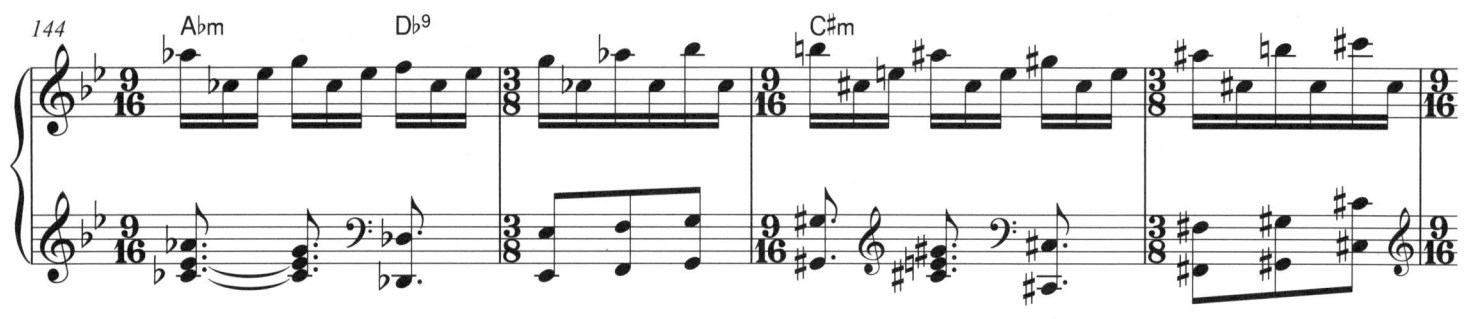

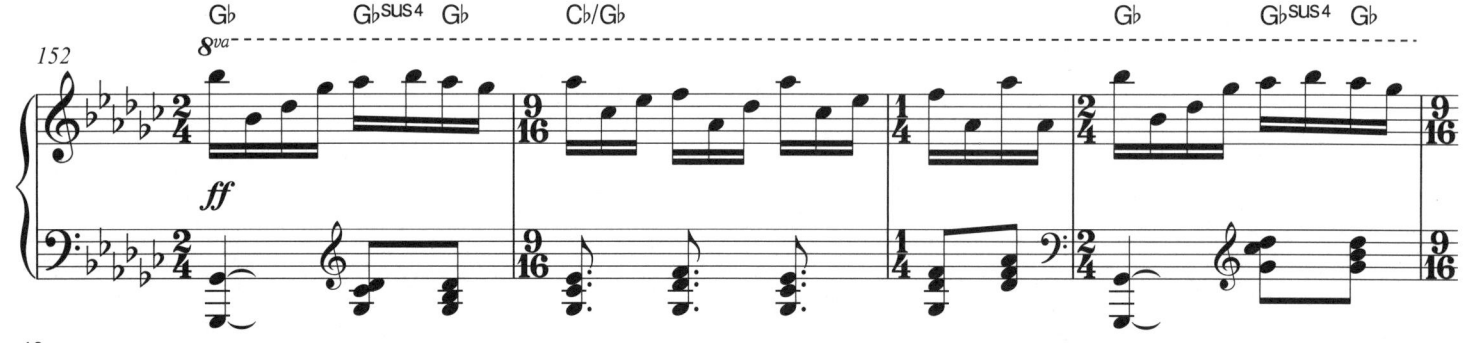

GRADE 08
KEYBOARDS

SINGLE BY
Nina Simone

ALBUM
Little Girl Blue

RELEASED
24 June 1958

RECORDED
**Late 1958, Beltone Studio
New York City, New York
USA**

LABEL
Bethlehem

WRITERS
**Gus Kahn
Walter Donaldson**

PRODUCERS
**Nine Simone
Irv Greenbaum (engineer)**

MY BABY JUST CARES FOR ME

NINA SIMONE

WORDS AND MUSIC: GUS KAHN/WALTER DONALDSON

The 'high priestess of soul', Nina Simone was born Eunice Waymon in Tryon, North Carolina. A singer, songwriter and pianist, her music incorporated soul, gospel, jazz, blues, folk, show tunes and classical influences. 'I Loves You, Porgy', taken from her debut album, was a US top-20 hit in 1959 and her recording was honoured with a Grammy Hall of Fame Award in 2000, three years before her death at the age of 70.

The song 'My Baby Just Cares for Me' was first heard in the 1930 American musical comedy film *Whoopee!*, which also introduced the jazz standard 'Makin' Whoopee'. Written by Walter Donaldson (music) and Gus Kahn (lyrics), Simone recorded another song of theirs, 'Love Me or Leave Me' for her 1958 debut album *Little Girl Blue*. Featuring jazz musicians Jimmy Bond on double bass and Albert 'Tootie' Heath on drums, the entire album was recorded in one 14-hour session, with 'My Baby Just Cares for Me' left to the end. It wasn't a hit single until its use in a TV advert for Chanel No. 5 perfume in 1987, after which it became a top-ten hit in several countries, including No. 5 in the UK and No. 1 in the Netherlands. Later, *Wallace and Gromit* makers Aardman Animations produced a popular claymation music video to accompany its release.

⚡ PERFORMANCE TIPS

This classic jazz song should, of course, be played with a piano sound. Aim to keep the right-hand chords light and the left-hand walking bass line detached but not staccato, like a double bass. The famous piano solo in the middle is split into two sections: one culminating in the right-hand triplet melody from bar 51 to the chord at the beginning of bar 53, and the other featuring a build-up of triplet chords at bars 65-67. Practise both slowly and gradually increase the speed, emphasising evenness in the triplets.

MY BABY JUST CARES FOR ME

WORDS AND MUSIC:
GUS KAHN/WALTER DONALDSON

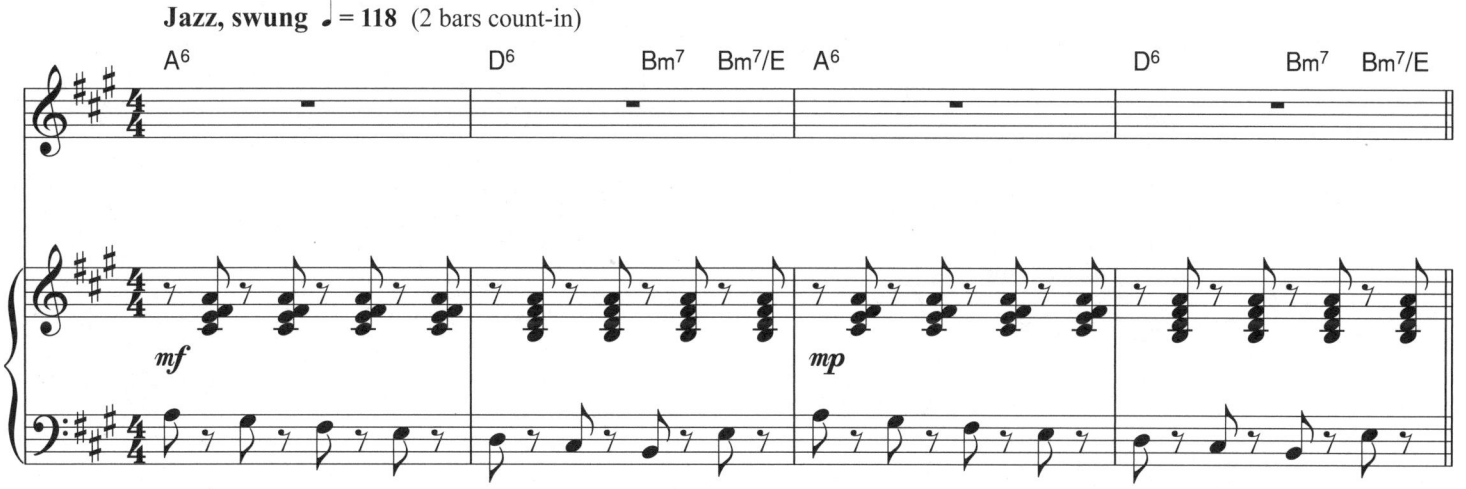

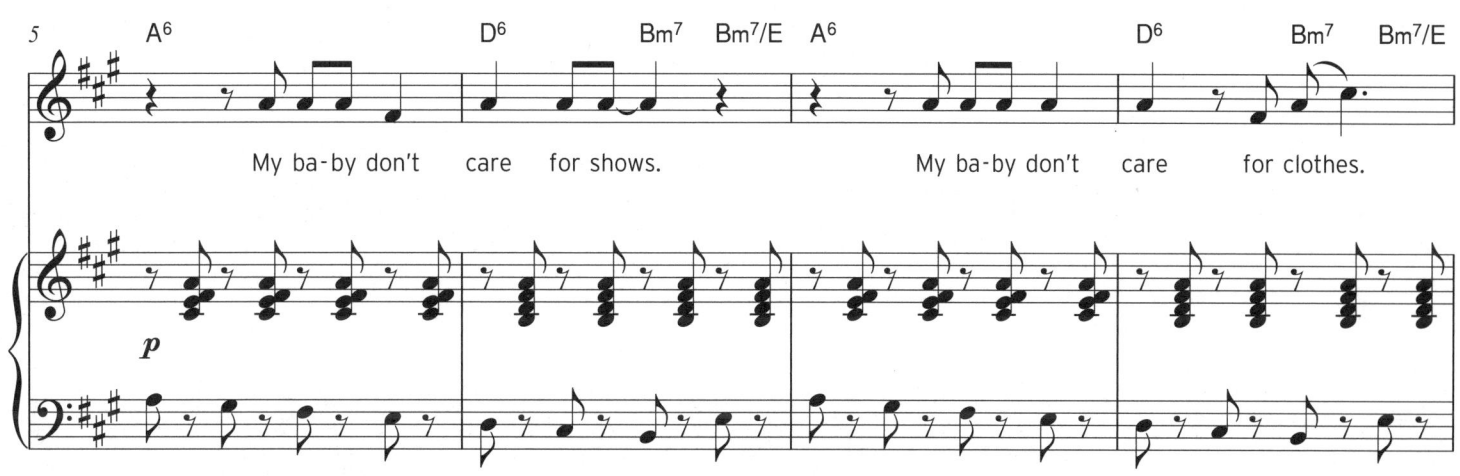

My ba-by don't care for shows. My ba-by don't care for clothes.

My ba-by just cares _____ for me.

© 1930 (Renewed 1958) Gilbert Keyes Music Company and Donaldson Publishing Company
All rights for Gilbert Keyes Music Compny administered by WB Music Corp.
Imagem Music/EMI Music Publishing Limited
All Rights Reserved. International Copyright Secured. Used by permission

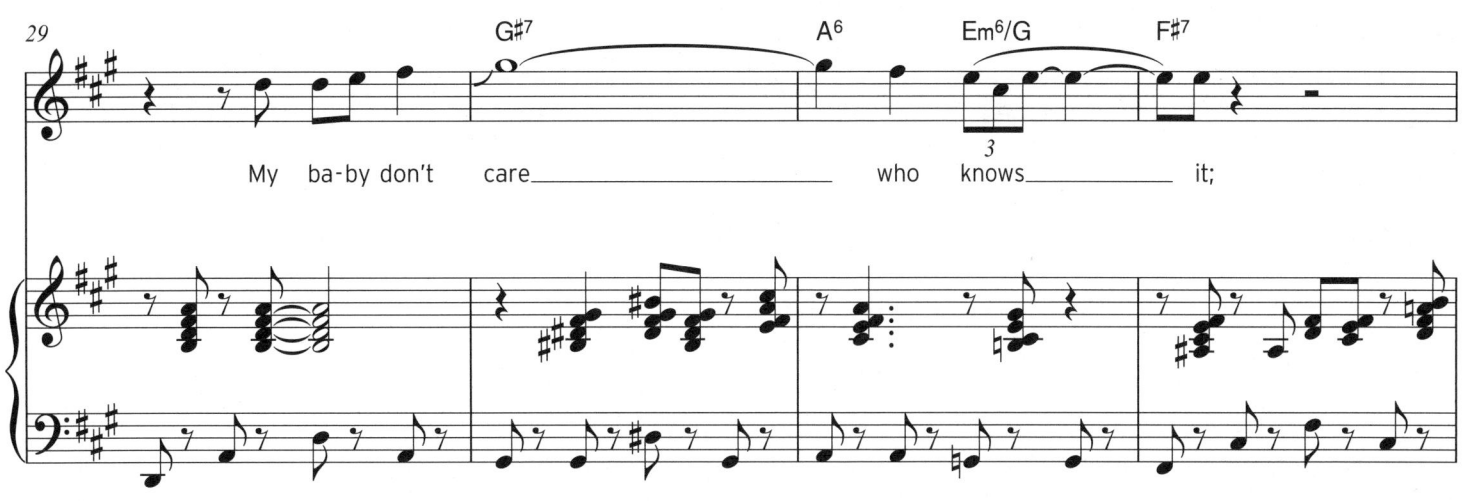
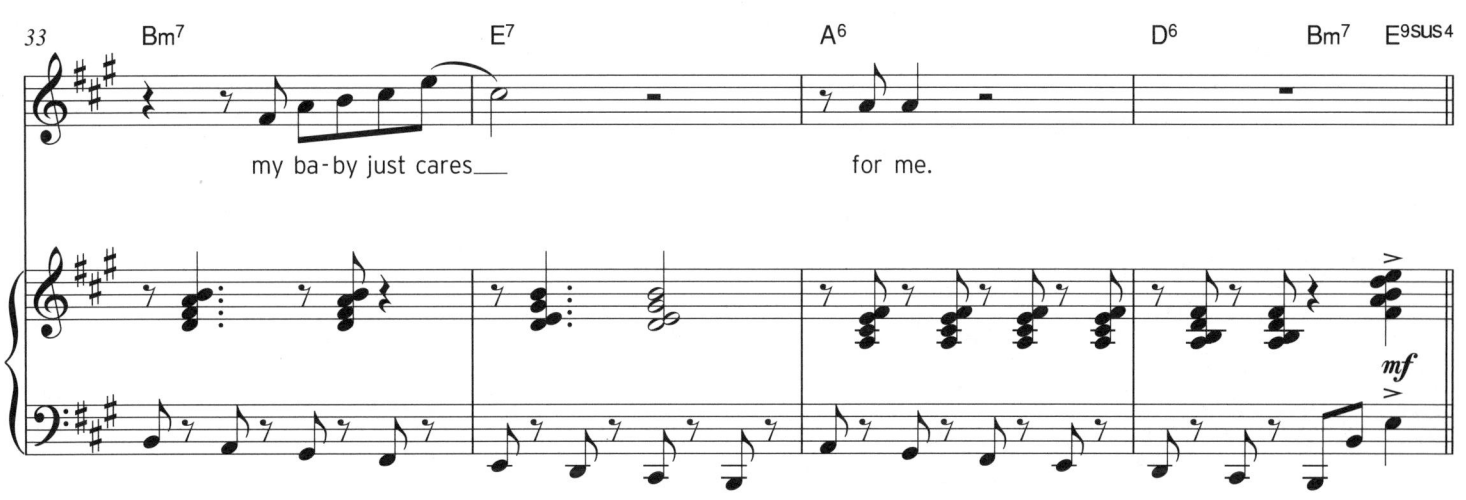

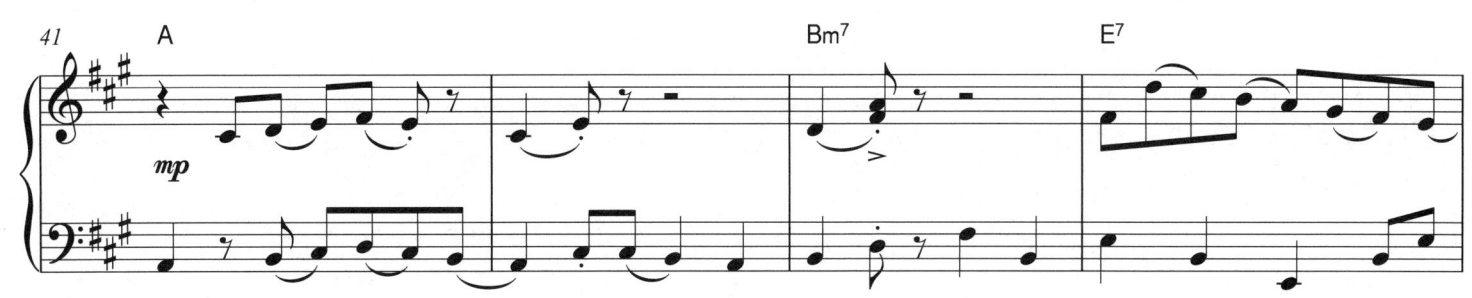

YOUR PAGE
NOTES

TECHNICAL FOCUS

PEACHES EN REGALIA
FRANK ZAPPA

WORDS AND MUSIC: FRANK ZAPPA

08 GRADE
KEYBOARDS

SINGLE BY
Frank Zappa

ALBUM
Hot Rats

B-SIDE
Little Umbrellas

RELEASED
10 October 1969 (album)
1970 (single)

RECORDED
18 July-30 August 1969
TTG, Los Angeles
California, USA

Sunset Sound
Los Angeles
California, USA

Whitney Studios
Gelndale, California, USA
(album)

LABEL
Bizarre

WRITER
Frank Zappa

PRODUCER
Frank Zappa

Born of Sicilian-Greek parentage in Baltimore, American musician Frank Zappa was a self-taught composer, guitarist, singer and producer whose 1966 debut *Freak Out!* with his band The Mothers of Invention was rock's first double concept album. Fusing a myriad of influences from classical to jazz, he was one of music's most singular, experimental and prolific artists.

The opening track on Zappa's second solo album (and seventh overall), 1969's *Hot Rats*, 'Peaches en Regalia' is widely recognised as a modern jazz fusion standard. Zappa plays guitar, bass and percussion on the track, which he also wrote and produced. It also features Ian Underwood of The Mothers of Invention on keyboard and woodwind instruments, a 16-year-old Shuggie Otis on bass and lauded drumming by Ron Selico. The album was dedicated to Zappa's son Dweezil, born a month before the album's release. Forty years later, Dweezil won a Grammy Award for his version of 'Peaches en Regalia', performed by his tribute act Zappa Plays Zappa. Reflecting on the piece's enduring popularity in 1980, Frank said: 'That's probably the ultimate across the board Frank Zappa song of all time. It's the only thing I've never heard anybody say they didn't like.'

TECHNICAL FOCUS

Two technical focus elements are featured in this song:

- Contrasting musical characteristics
- Semiquaver broken chords

This arrangement takes ideas from the many different instruments on the original track, so you'll need to try to imitate these and create **contrasting musical characteristics**. Examples include bars 20-31 (guitar and flute), which should sound fluent and agile, and bars 45-47 (woodwind), which should be as staccato as possible. The **semiquaver broken chords** in both hands at bars 32-24 pose a real challenge of coordination. This passage will benefit from slow practice, perhaps in different rhythms.

TECHNICAL FOCUS
PEACHES EN REGALIA

WORDS AND MUSIC: FRANK ZAPPA

© 1969 (Renewed) by The Zappa Family Trust All Rights Reserved. Reprinted by Permission
Reprinted by permission of Hal Leonard LLC

GRADE 08 KEYBOARDS

SINGLE BY
Muse

ALBUM
The Resistance

RELEASED
14 September 2009

RECORDED
September 2008–May 2009, Studio Bellini, Lake Como, Lombardy, Italy

LABEL
Warner Bros. Helium-3

WRITER
Matthew Bellamy

PRODUCER
Muse

EXOGENESIS: SYMPHONY PART 2 MUSE

WORDS AND MUSIC: MATTHEW BELLAMY

Formed in Teignmouth, Devon in 1994 by Matt Bellamy (vocals, guitar, piano), Chris Wolstenholme (bass) and Dominic Howard (drums), Muse have grown to become one of the world's biggest stadium bands. Fusing elements of prog rock, heavy metal, electronic, pop and classical music, they have had 22 top-40 hit singles and ten top-40 albums (including five No. 1s) in the UK between 1999 and 2016.

The climax to Muse's fifth studio album, 2009's *The Resistance*, the 'Exogenesis: Symphony' is a 13-minute sequence of orchestrated songs divided into three movements 'influenced by Rachmaninov, Richard Strauss, Chopin and Pink Floyd,' according to Bellamy. The band's frontman composed it over a number of years, the genesis for its creation dating back to the writing period for their 2003 album *Absolution* and further encouraged by his co-writing of the nine-minute end title theme for the 2009 film *The International*. Speaking about 'Exogenesis', he said: 'It's not orchestration you'd normally expect from a rock band and we've done all the arranging and scoring.' Bellamy's piano playing comes to the fore in Part 2 of the piece in the section titled 'Cross-Pollination'. The album topped the charts in many countries including the UK and earned the band their first Grammy Award in 2011 for Best Rock Album.

 PERFORMANCE TIPS

To prepare for the opening section of this song, try practising chromatic scales with both hands together in double octaves. Careful listening to the original track will also help, as the timing and phrasing – in particular bars 18-37 and bar 107 to the end – are expressive and idiosyncratic. You'll also need to adapt quickly to each new tempo and mood as it comes.

EXOGENESIS: SYMPHONY PART 2

WORDS AND MUSIC:
MATTHEW BELLAMY

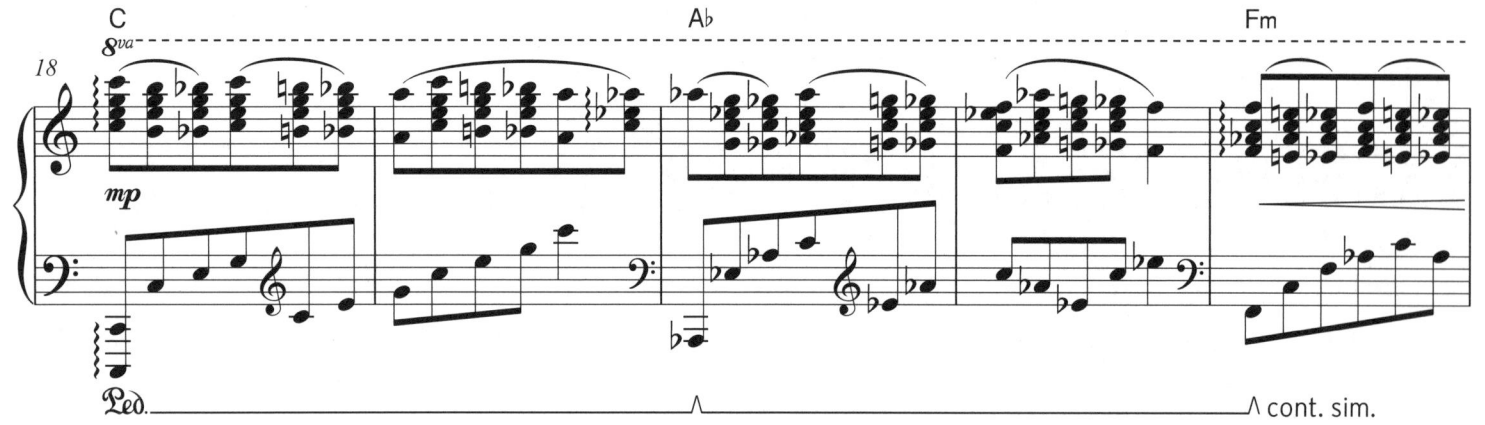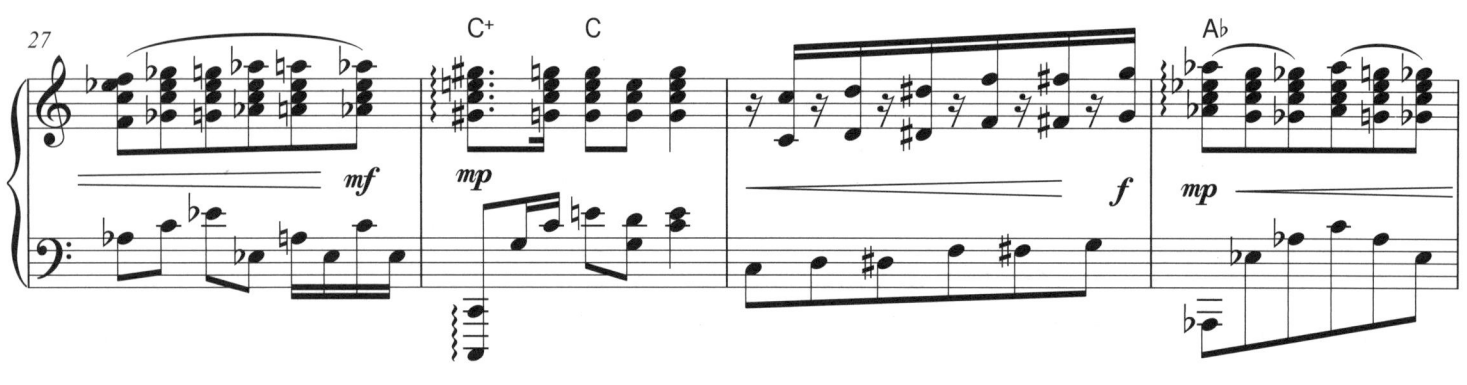

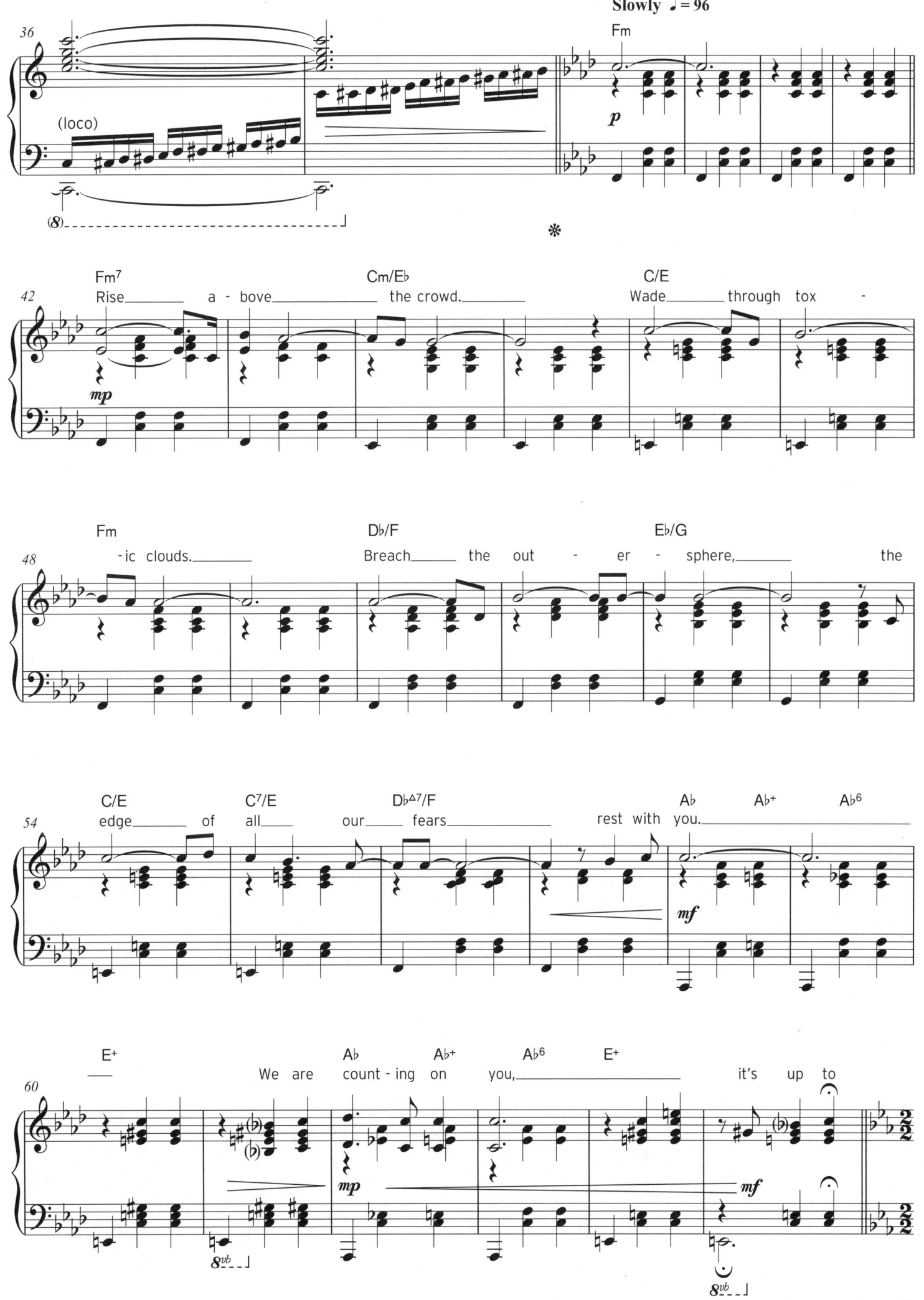

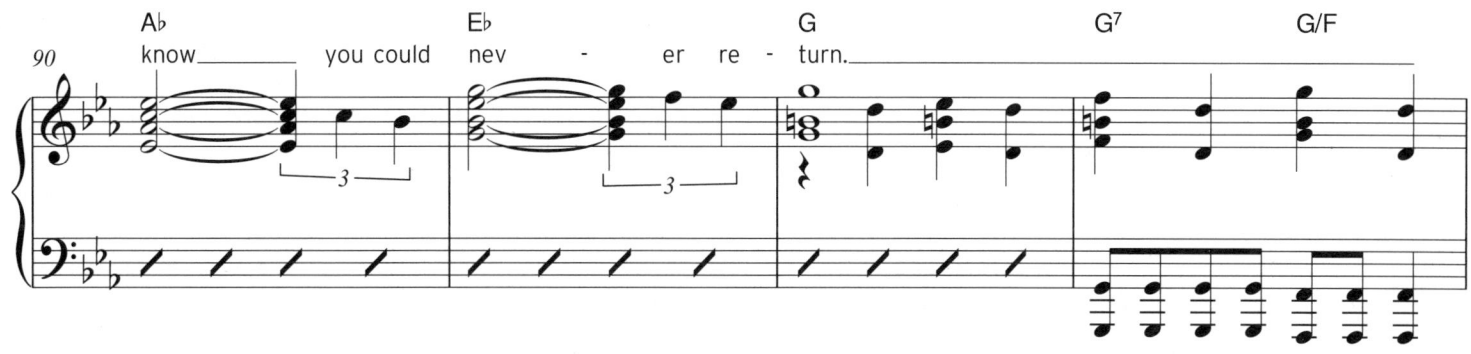

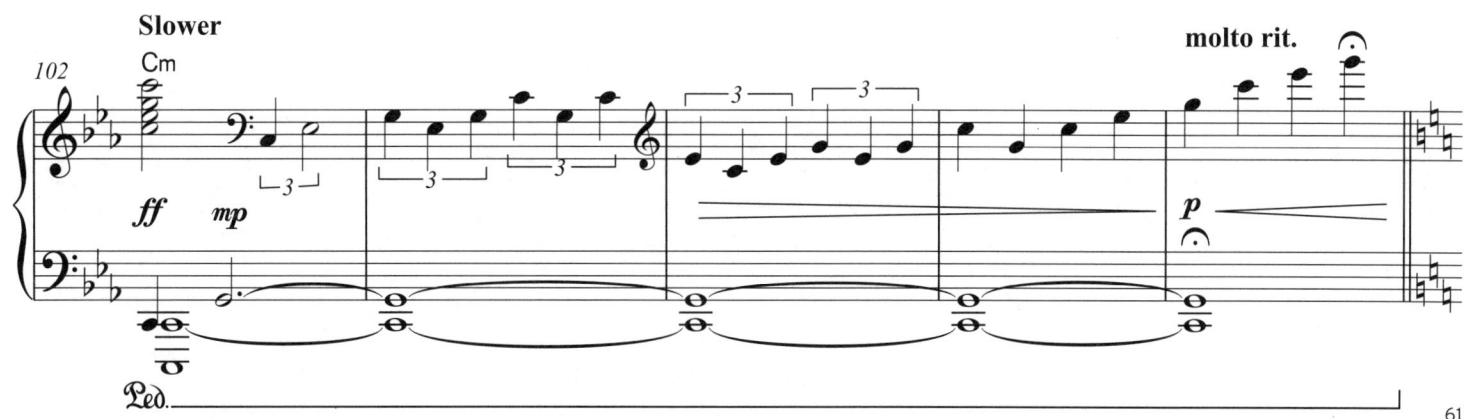

Tempo 1 (freely)

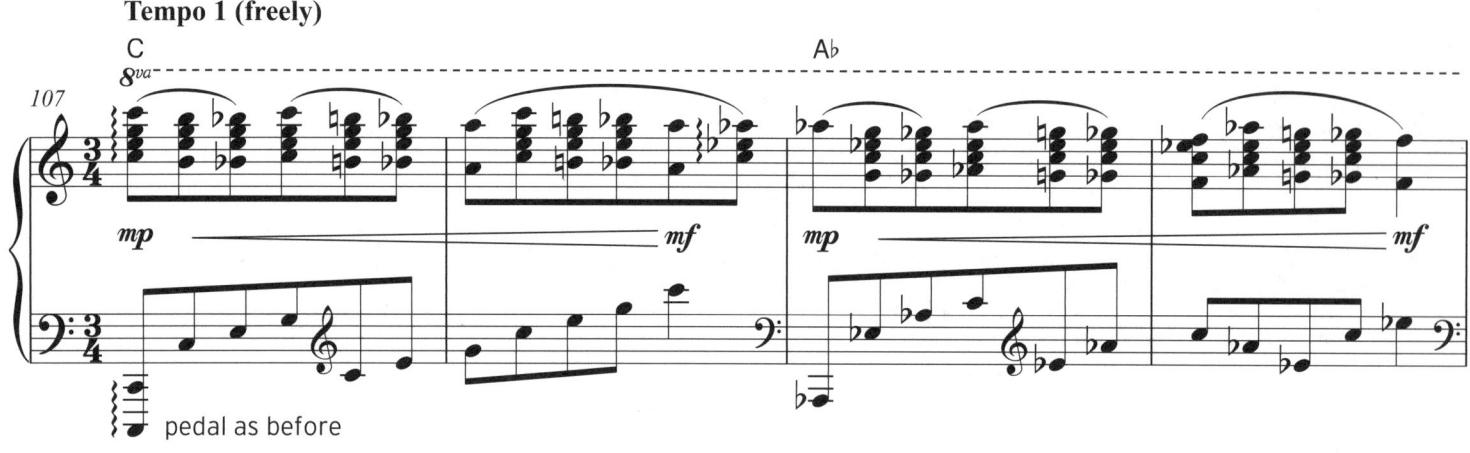
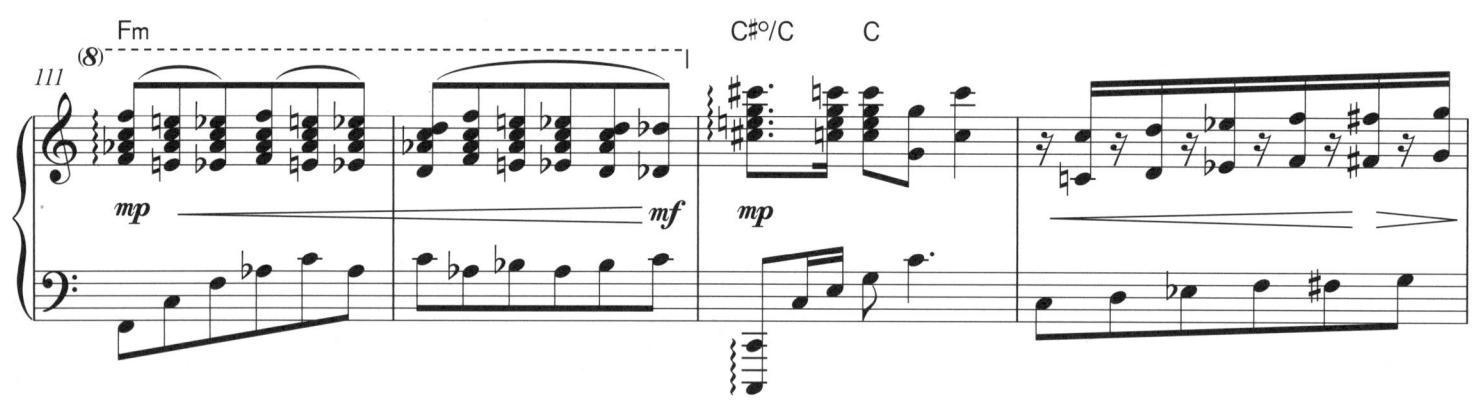

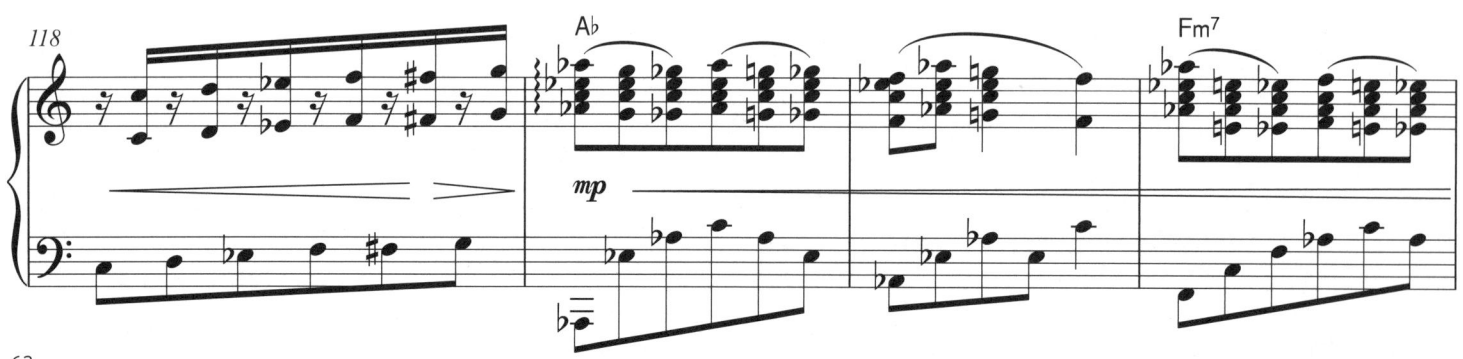

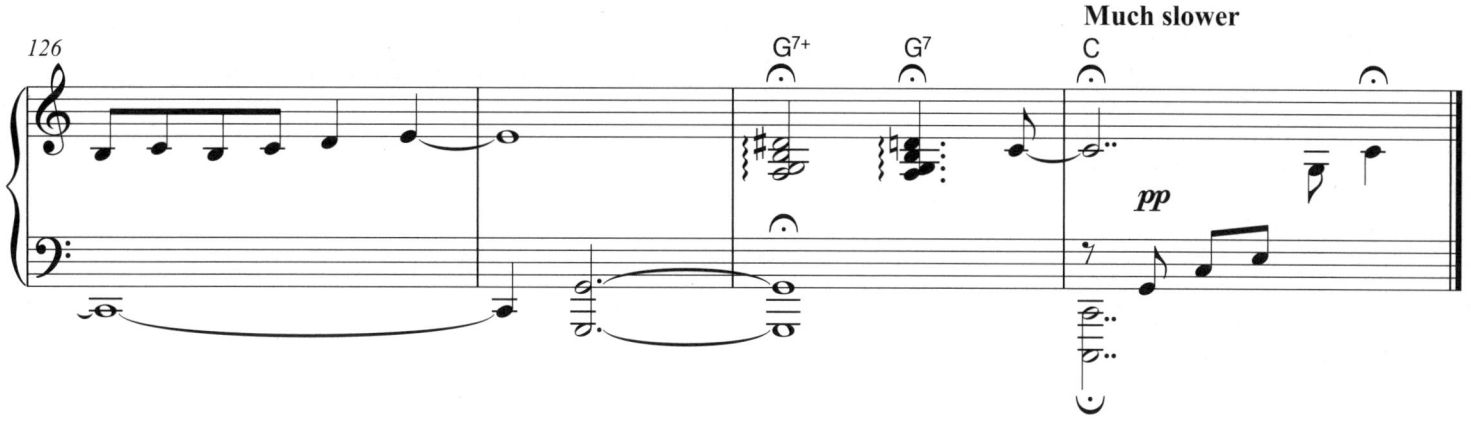

GRADE 08
KEYBOARDS

SINGLE BY
Snarky Puppy

ALBUM
Tell Your Friends

RELEASED
21 September 2010

RECORDED
21 November 2009, Dockside Studio, Maurice, Louisiana, USA

LABEL
Ropeadope

WRITER
Bill Laurance

PRODUCER
Michael League

TECHNICAL FOCUS

READY WEDNESDAY
SNARKY PUPPY

WORDS AND MUSIC: BILL LAURANCE

Snarky Puppy was formed by bassist and primary composer Michael League in 2003, beginning as a group of college friends at the University of North Texas Jazz Studies program and expanding three years later when they absorbed members of the Dallas gospel and R&B community. They are a culturally diverse instrumental collective with as many as 25 members in regular rotation.

After a decade of relentless touring and recording in all but complete obscurity, Snarky Puppy have found themselves acknowledged as one of the major forces in the jazz world. The band won their first Grammy Award in 2014 for Best R&B Performance, were voted Jazz Group of the Year by readers of *Down Beat* magazine in 2015, and won their second Grammy for Best Contemporary Instrumental Album in 2016. 'Ready Wednesday' is the nine-minute closing track of Snarky Puppy's fourth album, 2010's *Tell Your Friends*. The album was filmed and recorded live in one night at Dockside Studio in Maurice, Louisiana, in front of a 30-person studio audience. Founding member, pianist and composer of the piece Bill Laurance explains the title:

> The idea is that if you're not ready by Wednesday, then you never will be. Whenever I was at work or school, when it got to Wednesday I would say 'I'm ready to make stuff happen'.

TECHNICAL FOCUS

Two technical focus elements are featured in this song:

- Melody spread between the hands
- Articulation

Bars 5-16 feature the **melody spread between the hands** – for example, the repeated note E in the left hand is actually part of the right-hand phrase. You'll need to ensure that this effect sounds like one hand through careful coordination and tonal consistency. Note the **articulation** at bars 69-92, where the slurs were originally created with a pitch bend wheel. Emphasise the start of each slur to create interest in the melodic line.

TECHNICAL FOCUS
READY WEDNESDAY

WORDS AND MUSIC: BILL LAURANCE

Jazz fusion ♩ = 129 (2 bars count-in)

© Copyright 2010 GroundUp Music LLC/BMG Rights Management
All Rights Reserved. Printed by Permission

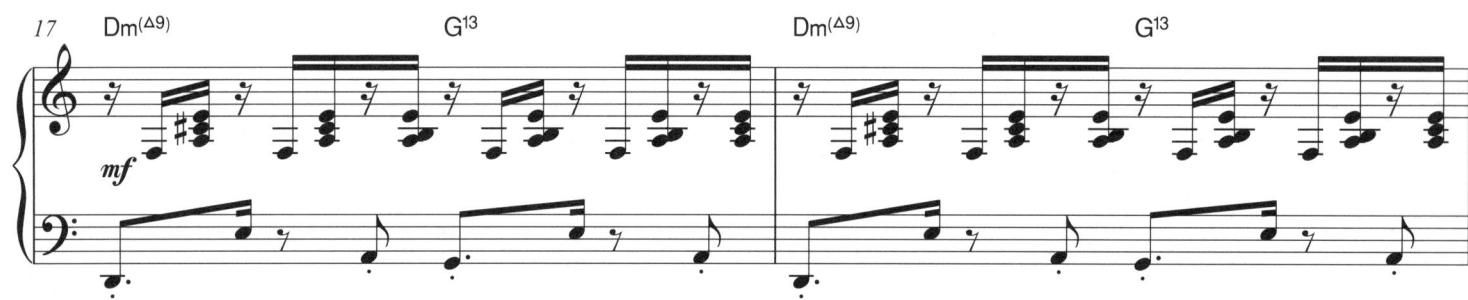
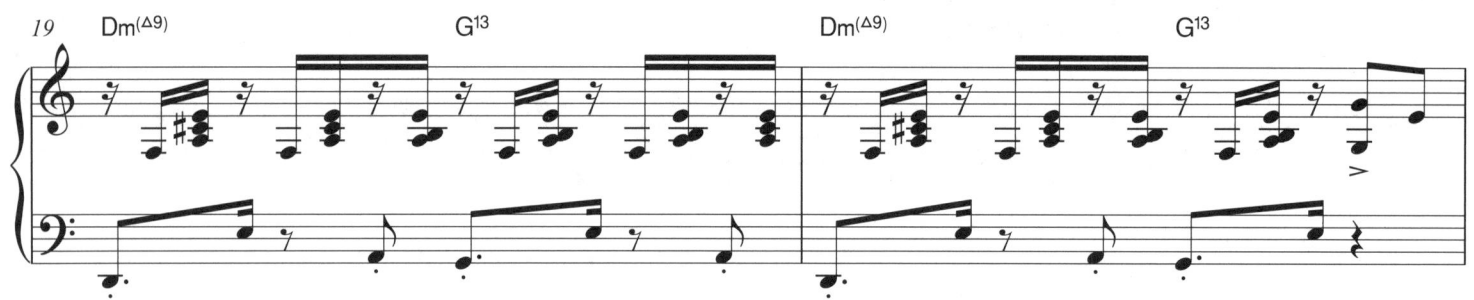
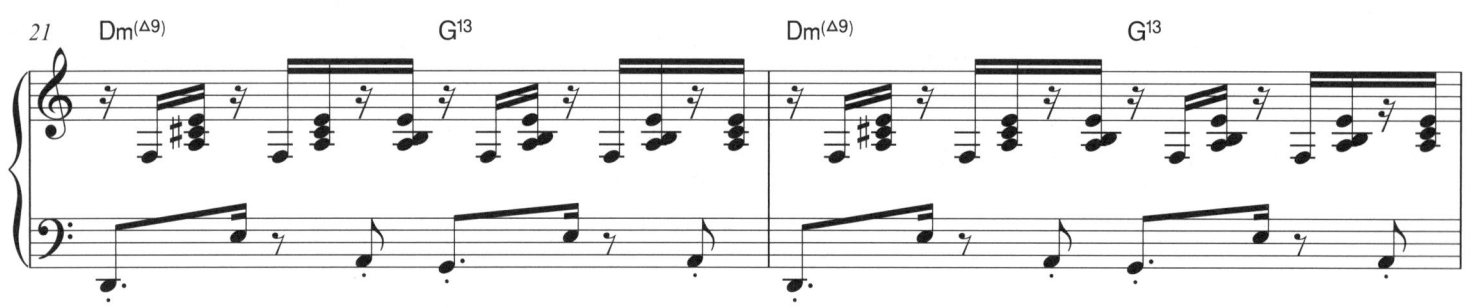

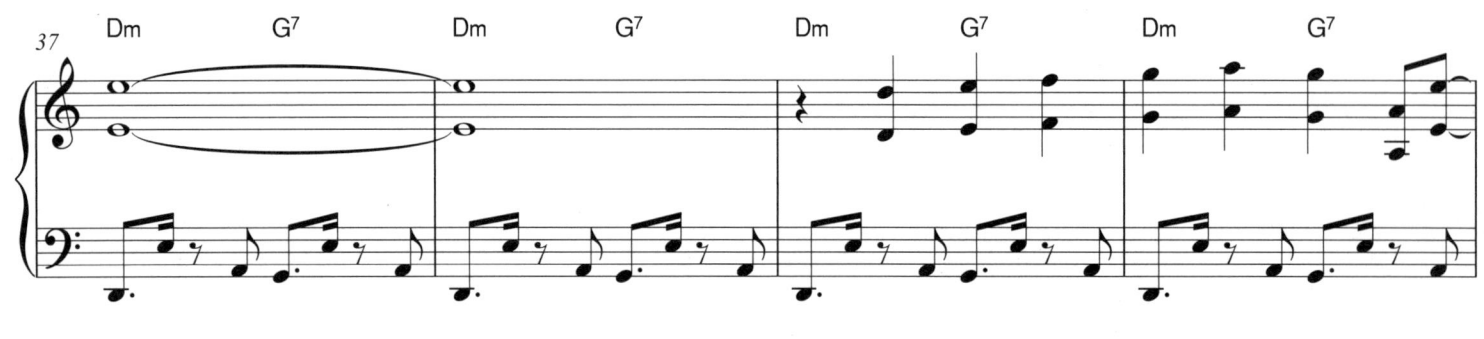

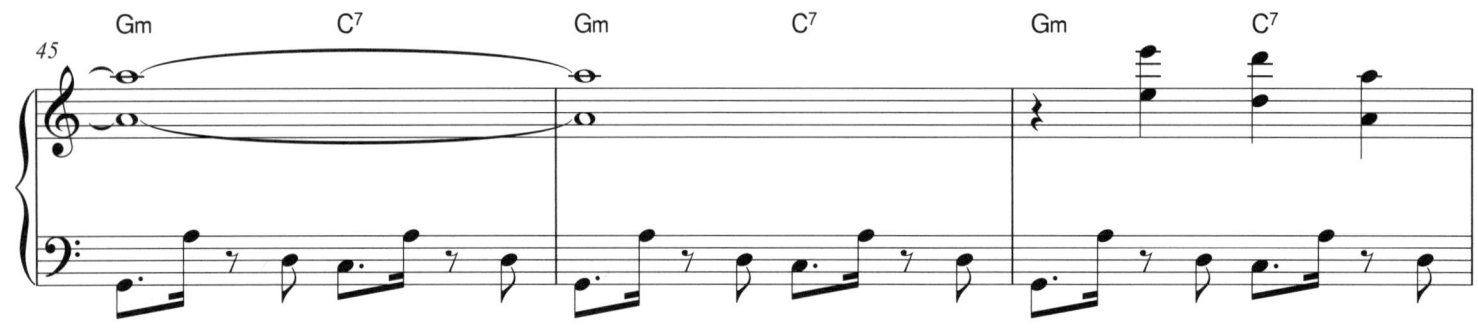
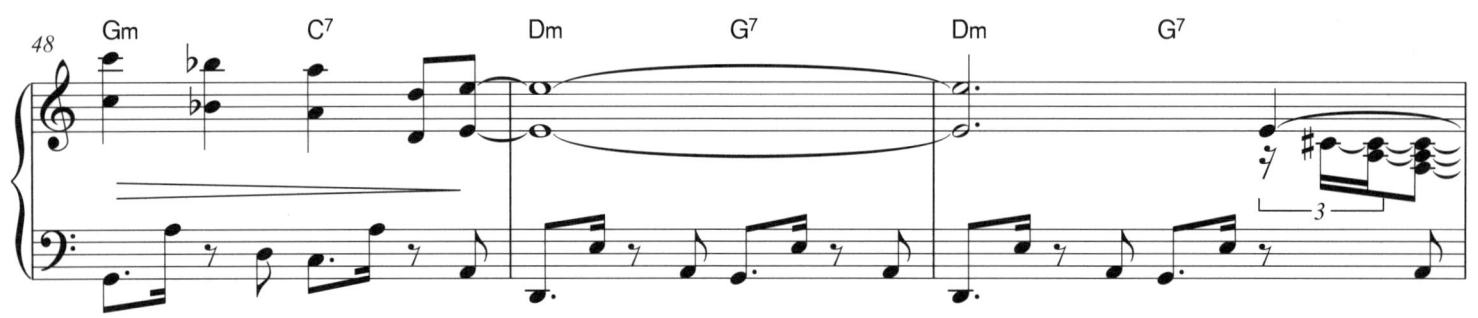
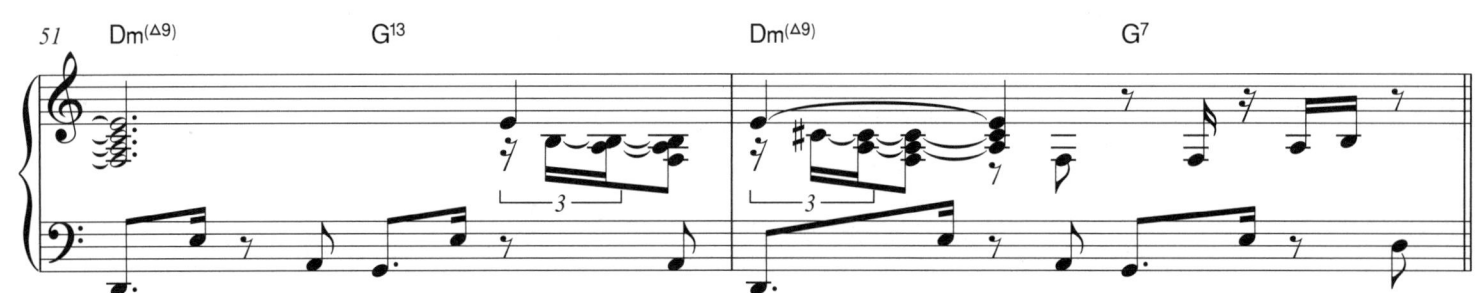

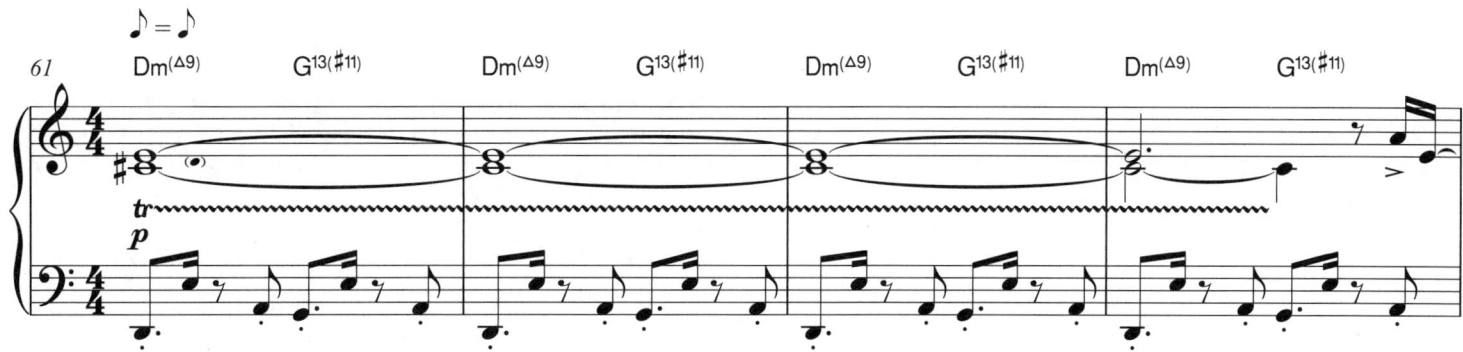

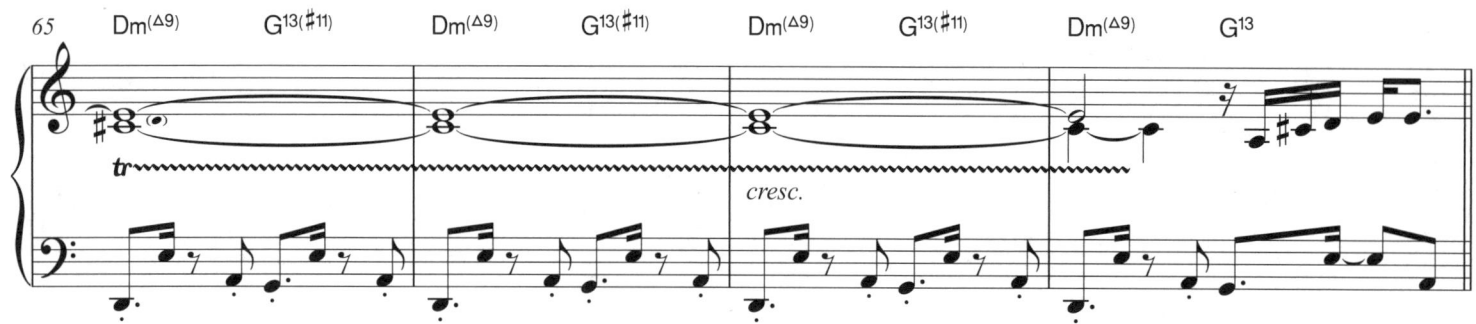

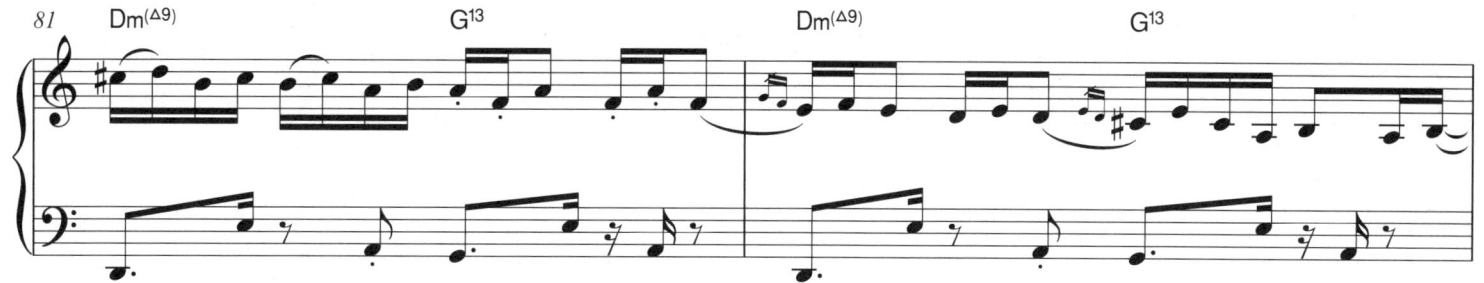
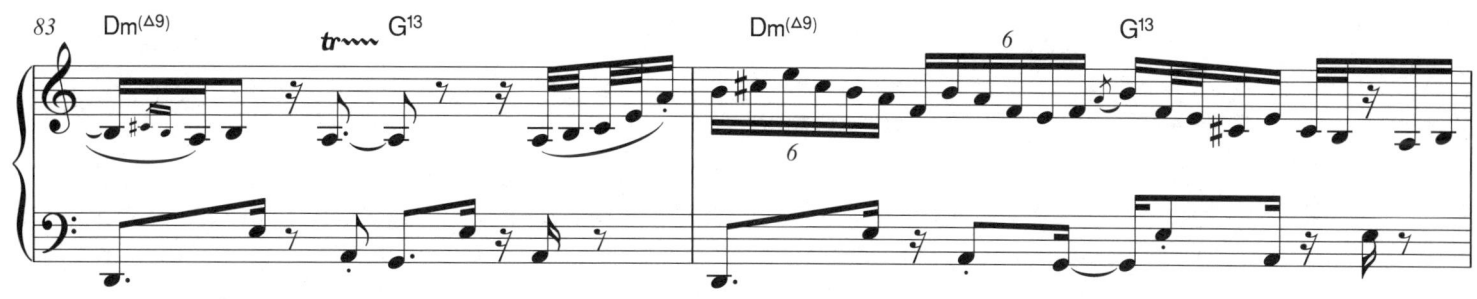

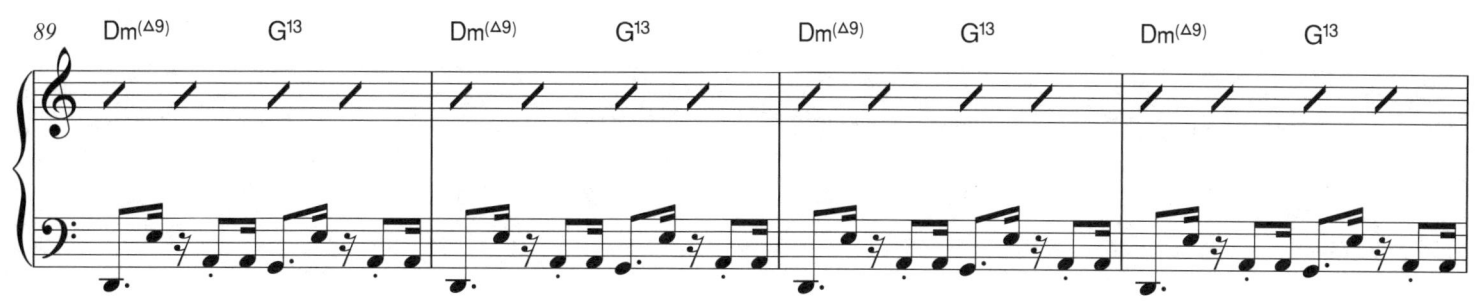

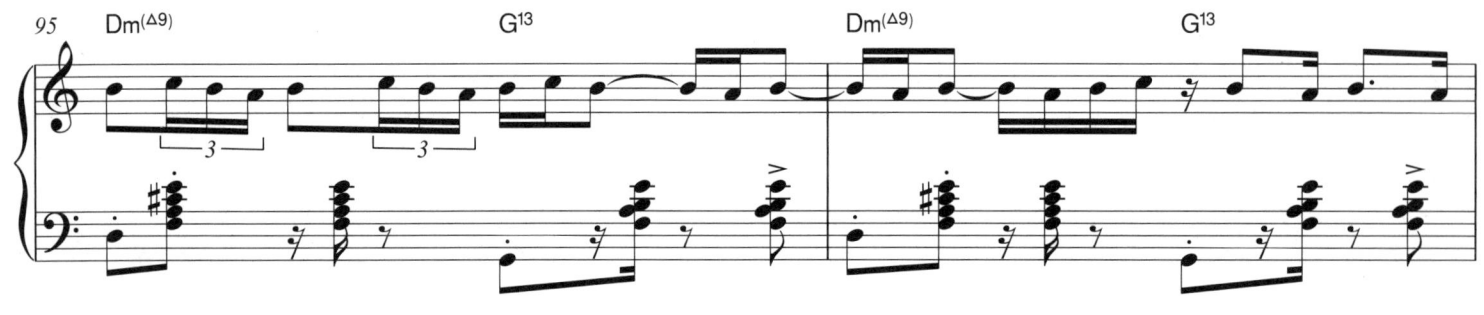
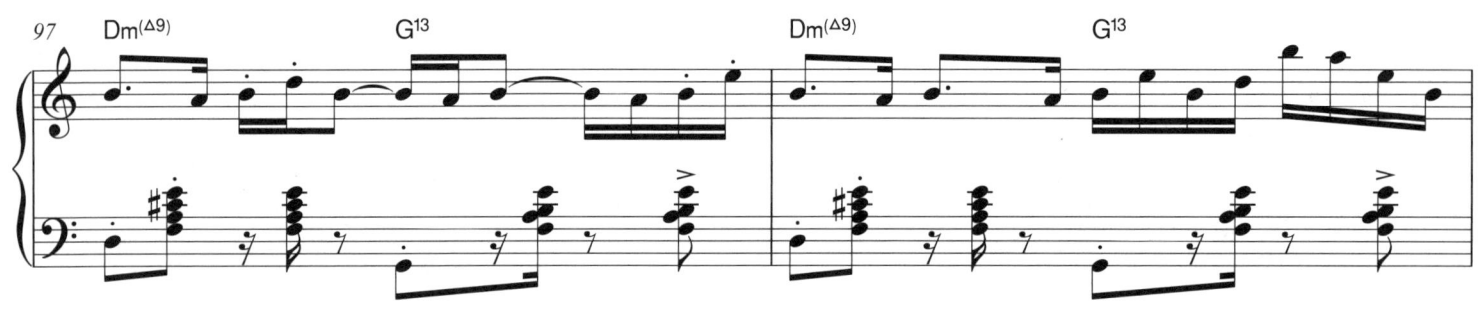
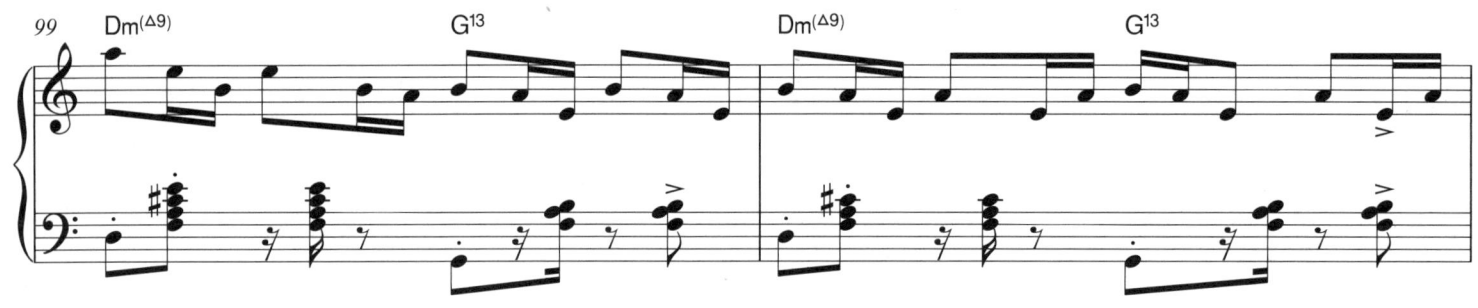
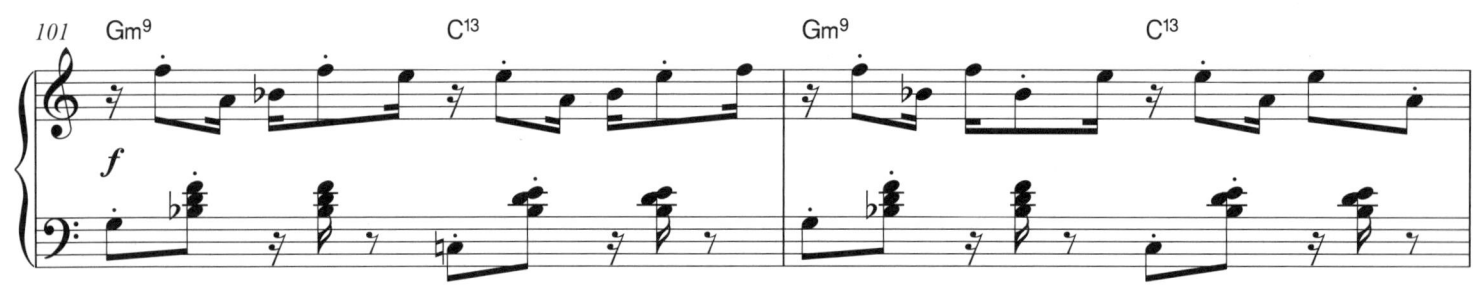
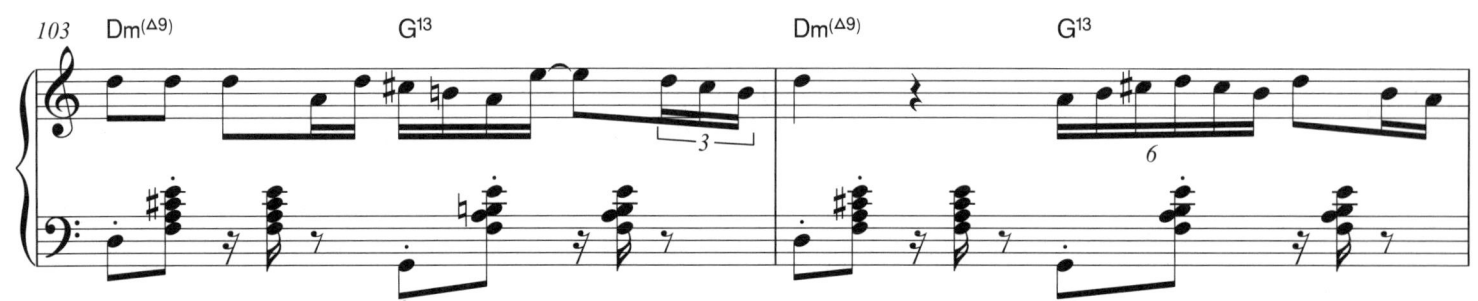

HELP PAGES

CHOOSING SONGS FOR YOUR EXAM

SONG 1

Choose a song from this book.

SONG 2

Choose a song which is:

Either a different song from this book

or from the list of additional Trinity Rock & Pop arrangements, available at trinityrock.com

or from a printed or online source

or your own arrangement

or a song that you have written yourself

You can play Song 2 unaccompanied or with a backing track (minus the keyboard part). If you like, you can create a backing track yourself (or with friends), add your own vocals, or be accompanied live by another musician.

The level of difficulty and length of the song should be similar to the songs in this book and match the parameters available at trinityrock.com
When choosing a song, think about:

- Does it work on my instrument?
- Are there any technical elements that are too difficult for me? (If so, perhaps save it for when you do the next grade)
- Do I enjoy playing it?
- Does it work with my other songs to create a good set list?

SONG 3: TECHNICAL FOCUS

Song 3 is designed to help you develop specific and relevant techniques in performance. Choose one of the technical focus songs from this book, which cover two specific technical elements.

SHEET MUSIC

If your choice for Song 2 is not from this book, you must provide the examiner with a photocopy. The title, writers of the song and your name should be on the sheet music. You must also bring an original copy of the book, or a download version with proof of purchase, for each song that you perform in the exam.

Your music can be:

- A lead sheet with lyrics, chords and melody line
- A chord chart with lyrics
- A full score using conventional staff notation

HELP PAGES

PLAYING WITH BACKING TRACKS

All your backing tracks can be downloaded from soundwise.co.uk

- The backing tracks begin with a click track, which sets the tempo and helps you start accurately
- Be careful to balance the volume of the backing track against your instrument
- Listen carefully to the backing track to ensure that you are playing in time
- Keyboard players should not use auto-accompaniment features for these exams as the aim is to play with a backing track

If you are creating your own backing track, here are some further tips:

- Make sure that the sound quality is of a good standard
- Think carefully about the instruments/sounds you are using on the backing track
- Avoid copying what you are playing in the exam on the backing track – it should support, not duplicate
- Do you need to include a click track at the beginning?

COPYRIGHT IN A SONG

If you are a singer, instrumentalist or songwriter it is important to know about copyright. When someone writes a song they automatically own the copyright (sometimes called 'the rights'). Copyright begins once a piece of music has been documented or recorded (eg by video, CD or score notation) and protects the interests of the creators. This means that others cannot copy it, sell it, make it available online or record it without the owner's permission or the appropriate licence.

COVER VERSIONS

- When an artist creates a new version of a song it is called a 'cover version'
- The majority of songwriters subscribe to licensing agencies, also known as 'collecting societies'. When a songwriter is a member of such an agency, the performing rights to their material are transferred to the agency (this includes cover versions of their songs)
- The agency works on the writer's behalf by issuing licences to performance venues, who report what songs have been played, which in turn means that the songwriter will receive a payment for any songs used
- You can create a cover version of a song and use it in an exam without needing a licence

There are different rules for broadcasting (eg TV, radio, internet), selling or copying (pressing CDs, DVDs etc), and for printed material, and the appropriate licences should be sought out.

YOUR
PAGE
NOTES

YOUR
PAGE
NOTES

YOUR PAGE
NOTES